CATHOLICISM IN AMERICA:
A SOCIAL HISTORY

by
Timothy Walch

AN ANVIL ORIGINAL

under the general editorship of
Louis L. Snyder

ROBERT E. KRIEGER PUBLISHING COMPANY
Malabar, Florida

1989

Original Edition 1989

Printed and Published by
ROBERT E. KRIEGER PUBLISHING COMPANY, INC.
KRIEGER DRIVE
MALABAR, FLORIDA   32950

Library of Congress Cataloging-in-Publication Data

Walch, Timothy, 1947–
    Catholicism in America : a social history/by Timothy Walch.—
Original ed.
        239p.   cm.—(Anvil series)
        "An Anvil original."
        Bibliography: p.
        Includes index.
        ISBN 0-89874-977-8 (alk. paper)
        1. Catholic Church—United States—History. 2. Sociology,
Christian (Catholic)—History. 3. Sociology, Christian—United
States—History. 4. United States—Church history. I. Title.
BX1406.2.W33 1989   88-9040
282'.73—dc19   CIP

10   9   8   7   6   5   4   3   2

DEDICATION

For Thomas Emmet Walch and Brian Edward Walch,
two chapters in the evolving story of American Catholicism.

TABLE OF CONTENTS

Chapter 9

THE AMERICAN CATHOLIC REVOLUTION,

Chapter 10

PART II
READINGS

PREFACE

A book such as this one is very much a collaboration. Foremost among the contributors are the dozens of scholars who have been writing about the history of American Catholicism over the past several decades; many of their ideas are reflected in the text and their works are cited in the bibliography at the end of the book. They share in any credit that is due this book.

In my research I found myself returning to the work of three scholars who are worthy of special mention. Professor Jay P. Dolan and the Reverend James Hennesey, S.J. have written companion histories of American Catholicism that are commended to any reader who wishes to explore the topic more deeply; their work exemplifies the very best in historical scholarship. Yet the major influence on this work can be traced to Monsignor John Tracy Ellis, the dean of American Catholic history. Through his classroom lectures and his many books Monsignor Ellis provided me with a deep and continuing appreciation of the American Catholic past. For that I will always be grateful.

I am also most grateful for the detailed comments on the manuscript of this book provided by several scholars. Joseph White of the Cushwa Center for the Study of Catholicism at the University of Notre Dame was most helpful in correcting some of my mistaken notions of nineteenth-century Catholicism. John L. Elias of Fordham University reviewed the manuscript from the perspective of a professor of religious education. Edward R. Kantowicz, formerly of Careleton University in Canada, was most gracious in providing a detailed critique of the manuscript; his imprint is on every chapter. I would also like to thank Louis L. Snyder and Ida Mae Brown Snyder for their many substantive and editorial contributions to the manuscript. Together, these colleagues have made a more readable and thoughtful book.

Above all, however, I would like to note the strong support for this project that I received from my wife, Victoria Irons Walch. She is my partner in faith and in life; without her encouragement, this book would not have been possible.

Part I

HISTORY OF
CATHOLICISM IN AMERICA

CHAPTER 1

THE CHALLENGES TO AMERICAN CATHOLICISM

America has always been a religious nation. From the jeremiads of the seventeenth-century Puritans to the daily invocations by chaplains of the U.S. Congress, Americans have repeatedly called on the Almighty to guide their nation. The motto "In God We Trust" appears on American coins, and the phrase "one nation under God" is part of the American pledge of allegiance. Most important, the U.S. Constitution guarantees the right of all Americans to practice their belief in God without fear of government interference.

It is not surprising, therefore, that many religious denominations have flourished in the United States. Virtually all of the world's religions are represented within the nation's borders. This is not to say that even the majority of these denominations are distinct in their cultural origins. Indeed, they are not. The majority of religious denominations in the United States are Protestant in origin and Protestantism has profoundly shaped the American national character. Even today, in an era of declining church attendance, America continues to be influenced by its Protestant roots.

Yet, ironically, though Protestantism has been and continues to be the dominant religious tradition in America, the Catholic Church has been the single largest denomination since the mid-nineteenth century. Today there are more than fifty-three million American Catholics, a number that represents between twenty and twenty-five percent of the population of the country.

This strength in numbers has given American Catholics little comfort over the past 137 years. Even though American Catholicism has prospered in terms of communicants, parishes, and social institutions, the Church rarely has been at ease in this country—at least not until recent times. The existing tension has been due in part to the periodic hostility of Protestants fearful that the Pope and his American followers were a threat to religious liberty. This alienation also has been due to an internal

1

struggle within the Catholic community over how an individual could be both American and Catholic. At various times throughout American history, both Catholics and non-Catholics have been concerned that the two philosophies were at odds.

THE CHALLENGE OF SURVIVAL. This tension has been exacerbated by a series of challenges faced by American Catholics over the past four centuries. The first—and some would say foremost—challenge was simple, physical survival in a hostile land. Beginning in 1565 with the first Catholic parish in Florida and for the next two centuries, Spanish priests worked to build missions and convert the Indians across the southern and western regions of what is now the United States. At the same time, French priests traveling south from Canada attempted to convert the Indians of what is now the northeastern and midwestern states.

To say that these missionary efforts were a struggle would be an understatement. Even in the best of times these men faced extraordinarily hard lives. Shortages of food, supplies, clothing, and shelter were common. Many of the Indian tribes tortured and killed the missionaries as if they were enemies. The tales of their deaths are gruesome, even by today's standards. "Large pieces were cut out of the bodies of both priests and roasted by the Indians,"* noted one typical account. It is not surprising that so many of these selfless priests have been canonized as saints of the Catholic Church.

Though Spanish and French missionaries were the first Catholics in America, their impact was severely limited by their small numbers and the general harshness of their world. To be sure, they explored and charted vast territories of the United States and converted hundreds of thousands of Indians to Christianity. But their foundations were not permanent, and by the 1760s, the missionary movement fell into decline. The lasting legacy of these men was a string of settlements and missions that would later become the sites for major American cities such as Chicago, Detroit, Los Angeles, San Antonio, and San Francisco, to name only a few.

---

*J. P. Dolan, *The American Catholic Experience* (Garden City, 1985) p. 37.

These zealous missionaries were not alone in their struggle to establish a Catholic beachhead on the American continent. Traveling from Britain in two small ships, a colony of English Catholics established a settlement in Maryland in 1634. Like their Spanish and French co-religionists these English Catholics suffered physical hardships due to the harshness of the environment and the hostility of Indian tribes. Yet Catholics in Maryland also suffered legal hardships and prejudice at the hands of their fellow Protestant colonists. By the end of the seventeenth century, most of the general assemblies of the English colonies in North America had approved legal restrictions against the practice of Catholicism; punishments for this "crime" ranged from fines, to imprisonment, to death.

In spite of the danger, the small colony of Maryland Catholics managed to survive and even to spread to nearby Pennsylvania. Other Catholics from Germany added to the size and diversity of the Pennsylvania Catholic community. As a defensive measure, however, Catholics in both Maryland and Pennsylvania largely isolated themselves from the mainstream of British colonial life. Colonial Catholics kept to themselves and their own kind, and only a few prominent Catholic families—the Carrolls for example—made much impact on public life in the British-American colonies.

The Revolution changed that to some extent. Religious prejudice still thrived, of course, but the Revolution led to the abolition of legal restrictions on religious freedom. In the afterglow of the Declaration of Independence, colonial assemblies passed new state constitutions that removed virtually all penalties on the practice of religion. By 1780, American Catholicism was no longer an underground religion.

Religious freedom also meant that Catholics had to redefine the place of their denomination in American society. For the first few decades after independence, Catholics argued among themselves over the substance of their religion and, more important, over who would lead the American branch of the Catholic Church—bishops, clergy, laity, or some combination of the three. Since 1634, American Catholicism had been led by the clergy and the laity working together informally in local parishes and congregations. The 1789 appointment of John Carroll as the first Catholic bishop in the United States, and the eventual appointment of other bishops shifted the balance of power from the laity and clergy to the bishops. Just as the American people sought checks and balances against excessive political power through their new Constitution, so also did American Catholics seek checks and balances against excessive episcopal power. Catholicism in the early years of the nineteenth century seemed to be consumed by petty power struggles and endless conflict.

THE CHALLENGE OF IMMIGRATION. The struggle for power within the American Church was aggravated by rapid and unrestrained growth. From about 1820 to 1930, 37.5 million European immigrants poured into the United States. Impoverished and illiterate for the most part, many of these new arrivals were Catholics who sought material assistance and spiritual nourishment from their religion.

The leaders of the American Church were not prepared for this invasion and lacked the resources to assist millions of new Catholics. Who would raise the funds and build the churches needed for these new Catholics? Where were the priests and nuns needed to care for these poor souls? It was clear to any priest who accepted the call to the episcopacy that the care of immigrant Catholics would be the preoccupation of his career.

Adding to the bishops' problems was the fact that these new Catholics were not docile supplicants, grateful for whatever assistance could be provided. For most of these new Catholics, religion was close to the heart, a mixture of Old World culture and Roman liturgy. It was important for immigrants, therefore, that their priests be of their own nationality, that their sermons and other prayers be conducted in their native language, and that their parishes and schools be devoted to the preservation of native culture. These new Catholics were not shy about expressing their desires to their new bishops.

This century of immigration was virtually unbroken except for the Civil War years, 1860-1865. Yet there are distinctions to be made between the first decades of immigration in comparison with the last decades. The first wave of immigrants, from 1820 to the Civil War and from 1870 to the mid-1880s, was predominantly Irish and German in origin. The Irish tended to favor American ways, while the Germans tenaciously held on to their native culture. A second wave of immigrants, from the mid-1880s through the 1920s, came from southern and eastern Europe. These Catholics shared with the Germans a desire to preserve traditional European cultures. Thus throughout the nineteenth and early twentieth centuries, "American" Catholicism was essentially a patchwork of distinct cultures loosely held together by a Roman liturgy and a common faith.

A common religious faith was not enough to make Catholics of different nationalities trust one another. Long after the power struggles of the early nineteenth century had been forgotten, conflict and argument within the Church were still major problems. The acrimonious din had not abated by the end of the century. It was not uncommon for the Irish to refer to German Catholics as "damned Dutchmen" and for the Germans to respond with a guttural "Irisher lump." Thus whenever the corps of predominantly Irish-born bishops in the United States sought to exert their episcopal authority over various national groups, the end result often was rebellion. At times there seemed to be very little Christianity within American Catholicism.

Church leaders had to cope with the massive growth within their denomination and win the confidence of distrustful, suspicious immigrants so as to shape them into a unified religious body. Building a denomination that was both decidedly American and distinctly Catholic from a multicultural, multilingual flock was no small task. Indeed, the bishops largely failed in their goal. Throughout the century of immigration, internecine contests for power between different church factions were common in almost every diocese. American Catholicism in the first decades of the twentieth century was not yet one denomination with one identity.

THE CHALLENGE OF AMERICANIZATION. Congress ended massive immigration to the United States with the passage of an immigration quota act in 1924, but the Congress did little to address the challenge of transforming the new arrivals or their children into American citizens. This task was left to the schools, the social service agencies, and the churches. Because the largest percentage of these foreigners were Catholic, the Church was deeply involved in the Americanization process. "It might, indeed, be maintained," noted Henry Steele Commager in his classic work *The American Mind,* "that the Catholic Church was during this period one of the most effective of all agencies for democracy and Americanization."* Yet this Americanization process would take several generations to show results.

At the turn of the twentieth century, Catholics of all nationalities clung to their native cultures and traditions with a fierce loyalty that frustrated almost all of the Church's efforts at Americanization. It was not until the 1910s, when the loyalty campaigns of World War I required every American to shed all things foreign, that Americanization began to take hold.

However, Americanization was not merely the simple act of abandoning old world traditions; Catholics needed a new identity, a way of defining what it meant to be both American and Catholic. Not only did Church leaders have to break down the walls separating one ethnic group from another, but also had to break down the barriers separating Catholics from the rest of American society.

This disassembly and reconstruction took time—two generations, two world wars, and an ecumenical council all contributed to the process. Beginning in the 1910s, and continuing to the 1960s, American Catholics of all nationalities gradually shed their cultural ties to Europe and became "American" in the true sense of the term. First went the foreign language parochial school, then the national parish, and later intermarriage between Catholics and different ethnic groups became increasingly common. By 1940 the internal walls separating Catholic ethnic groups from one another were crumbling with surprising speed.

World War II helped to break down the social barriers between Catholics and non-Catholics. Placed in military units without regard to their religion, many young Catholics met and befriended Protestants and Jews for the first time in their lives. The experience of combat established a bond between

*Henry Steele Commager, *The American Mind: An Interpretation of American Thought and Character Since the 1880s* (New Haven, CT, 1950) p. 193.

soldiers regardless of their faith. These young veterans did not quickly forget that fact.

Postwar residential patterns reflected this open-minded attitude. It was increasingly common in the 1940s and 1950s to find Catholics living in suburbs with neighbors of all faiths. After a brief spate of Catholic-Protestant tension in the late 1940s, Catholics and Protestants began a dialogue at the national level that helped to resolve long-term misunderstandings between these major denominations. The fruits of this dialogue were demonstrated in the election of a Catholic president and in the ecumenical declarations of the Second Vatican Council. By the mid-1960s, the process of Americanization was complete.

CONCLUSION. During the years after Vatican II, American Catholics have struggled not so much with their national identity as with their theology. Vatican II had raised doubts about the Faith in the minds of millions of Catholics; hundreds of thousands abandoned the Church altogether and tens of thousands of priests and nuns left their religious ministries. Those Catholics who stayed often ignored the leadership of their pastors, their bishops, and even their Pope. By the late 1960s, American Catholicism had been turned upside down.

Over the past twenty years American Catholics have struggled with their most recent challenge—to define the proper balance between the right to religious self-determination and the obligation to accept and follow the teaching authority of the Church. Should American Catholics follow their consciences or their Church on matters of faith and morals? It is a question that continues to generate controversy as American Catholicism enters its third century.

The chapters that follow chronicle the struggle of Catholics in America to address each of these challenges. It is a story of physical survival and conflict—conflict not only between Catholics and Protestants, but also among Catholics themselves. It is the story of the arduous process of immigration, economic mobility, and the slow process of becoming American. It is one aspect of the complex meaning and the genius of religious freedom in America.

CHAPTER 2

CATHOLICISM IN THE NEW WORLD, 1565–1784

Catholicism is one of the oldest European religious traditions in North America. As early as 1565, Spanish priests traveling with the explorer Juan Ponce de Léon established a parish at St. Augustine in Florida—the first of many Catholic settlements that would ring the United States in the two centuries before American independence.

From 1565 to 1784, wave after wave of Spanish and French missionary priests preached the gospel to the many and varied tribes of American Indians in what is now the United States. The hardship and deprivation suffered by these men was extraordinary but they believed that they were doing God's work in a new territory uncorrupted by sin. These priests believed that Christianity would flourish among the "noble savages" of the so-called "New World."

The Spanish focused their missionary efforts on the South. Florida settlements came first in 1565, followed by missions in what is now New Mexico at the end of the sixteenth century, Texas and Arizona in the seventeenth century, and California in the eighteenth century. Major American cities such as San Antonio, Santa Fe, San Diego, Los Angeles, and San Francisco all trace their origins and their names to Spanish missions.

Spanish priests were not alone in their quest. The famous French "black robes" fanned out from Quebec in Canada to learn from and educate the Indians of what is now the northeastern and midwestern United States. Like their Spanish counterparts, French priests were partly responsible for the foundation of dozens of settlements that later became American towns and cities. Detroit, St. Louis, New Orleans, and Mobile, among others, all have French origins.

THE SPANISH MISSION SYSTEM. In their attempt to dominate and civilize the Indians, the Spanish devised what became known as the "mission system." Under this system, the Spanish government provided financial support and physical protection for a series of small settlements to be established and administered by the Catholic Church. The overall purpose of the mission system was to transform these nomadic Indian tribes into a stable, docile work force that could be used for the benefit of the Spanish empire. The specific purpose of each mission was to provide religious instruction to the Indians, but missionary priests also taught cooking, sewing, weaving, farming, housing, cattle ranching, and other activities. In the absence of civil authorities, missionaries also served as agents of the Spanish government.

The mission system proved only partially successful. It did allow Spanish priests to minister to the Indians, break many of the tribes of their nomadic tendencies, and make some of them loyal subjects of the Spanish crown. However, the vast majority of Indians spurned the civilizing efforts of the Church, rejected the notion of living within the shadow of the missions, and asserted their independence from Spanish authority. The influence of the missions also was limited by the small number of priests who were willing to take up such a ministry. Even though the Spanish failed in their goal of converting the majority of the Indians, their missions were important and visible symbols of the Spanish Catholic presence in the New World.

Although the Spanish held high hopes for their first mission at St. Augustine, it never flourished. *(See Reading No. 1.)* Early records document the hardship and poverty of the Florida frontier; shipments of food and other provisions from Cuba and Mexico, for example, arrived on such an infrequent and irregular basis that local priests had no bread or wine to celebrate Mass for months at a time. A measure of success did come in the late 1590s, however, when Father Francisco Marron undertook a final effort to sustain a mission system in Florida. Unlike his predecessors, Marron succeeded in establishing two series of mission settlements—one along the east coast of Florida up into Georgia and a second northwest of St. Augustine to Apalachia Bay.

In spite of Marron's best efforts, however, the Florida mission system was a failure. One major problem was the Spanish civil authorities who abused the Indian population by exploiting it as a source of slave labor. Spanish troops savagely crushed a tribal revolt in 1656 and the incident destroyed all trust between the Indians, the missionaries, and the civil government. Another, more serious, threat to the Florida missions was the arrival of the English in America. The Protestant English and the Catholic Spanish clashed repeatedly and war between England and Spain from 1702 to 1713 threatened the very survival of St. Augustine as a Spanish colony. The war left the Florida missions in total disarray, never to recover.

The early years of the New Mexico mission system from 1598 to 1630 were very different from the formative years in Florida. To be sure, New Mexico missionaries suffered many of the same hardships, but they were blessed with a more receptive audience. The Pueblo Indians, a sedentary people, had a strong cultural interest in religion and they responded to the Christian gospel preached by the friars. By 1630, the superior of the New Mexico missions proudly reported that ninety friars had converted fifty thousand Pueblos over the previous three decades.

In spite of the hopes of these missionaries, these conversions did not create a permanent foundation. As was the situation in Florida, Spanish civil authorities in New Mexico enslaved the Indians, seized Indian lands, and granted this property to newly arrived Spanish colonists. The Pueblos struck back in 1680 and were successful in pushing Spanish religious and civil authorities out of Pueblo lands and into Texas. Four hundred Spaniards, including twenty-one priests died in this rebellion. The Spanish did not return to New Mexico until 1692, and the mission system never recovered.

Texas was a lost cause for the Spanish missionaries almost from the start. Unlike the Pueblos of New Mexico, the Indians of Texas were nomadic and sparsely settled. Try as they might, the missionaries could make few converts among the Apaches and the Comanches. Ironically, one of the most recognized symbols of the entire Spanish mission system is in Texas. Founded in 1718, the military post and mission of San Antonio de Valero in east central Texas would later become famous as the "Alamo," where Davy Crockett and hundreds of Texans lost their lives fighting for Texas independence. Outside of San Antonio, few missions survived in Texas.

If efforts in Texas can be categorized as a failure, the Arizona missions were a qualified success. This achievement was due in large part to one man—the Italian Jesuit, Eusebio Kino. (*See Reading No. 3.*) This legendary missionary arrived in Arizona in 1687 to work among the Pima Indians. Kino succeeded where others had failed because he accepted the Pima on their own terms. He did not try to force Catholicism on these Indians as many missionaries did. Instead, Kino quietly introduced a number of improvements in the quality of Pima life. Simple innovations such as cattle ranching and the introduction of new grains of wheat and fruit improved the Pima diet without undermining their culture.

The Pima came to accept, admire, and even to love Kino. They accepted his Catholicism precisely because he had helped them without any expectation of reciprocation. Other Jesuits found it difficult to carry on Kino's work. Even though the Pima embraced Father Kino, they were not receptive to other Jesuits. A small contingent of Jesuits continued to work in Arizona until the 1760s, but Kino's experiment among the Pima never flourished after his death in 1711.

Just as the success of the Arizona missions was dependent on one man, so also was the success of the California missions dependent on a single individual. Yet Father Junipero Serra, a Franciscan, was very different from Eusebio Kino. Kino had been an anthropologist, an explorer, and a cartographer. Serra was none of these; in fact, Serra's great strength was as an organizer and administrator. (*See Reading No. 4.*) During his fifteen years in California from 1769 to 1784, Serra founded nine missions along the coast from San Diego to San Francisco. It is interesting to note that this growth on the West Coast was taking place at the same time that Catholics and other colonists were caught up in the revolution that would lead to American independence from Britain.

The success of the mission system in California was due to a number of factors. To be sure, Junipero Serra was the most important, but he was not the only one. Serra was able to gather around him a number of experienced, committed priests to staff each of his missions. So also, the California climate was conducive to raising cattle, growing fruit, and cultivating grapes for wine. Finally, the Indians of California were less hostile to the Spanish than the Indians of the Southwest; in fact, they were very responsive to the overtures of Father Serra and his colleagues and the system continued into the nineteenth century.

For Spain and for the Church, the California missions were an economic wonder. The use of Indian labor and the favorable climate allowed the missionaries to cultivate a vast quantity of land. The fruit, wine, and beef from California were among the best in the world, but the price was high. The hard labor required of the Indians killed off the population and the decline of the mission system in California followed the demise of the Indian population.

FRENCH PRIESTS AND EXPLORERS. As Spanish missionaries pushed north from Mexico into the southwestern and western regions of the United States, French missionaries moved down from Canada into New England and the Midwest. In superficial ways, French missionary activities seemed quite similar to the Spanish mission system. Both efforts were administered jointly by church and government officials, and both efforts were dependent on the establishment of missions in strategic locations among the Indian tribes. Beyond these superficial similarities, the French missionary experience was very different from that of the Spanish. The French were not as committed to the New World as the Spanish, so fewer missionaries meant fewer mission stations and fewer conversions. The French sought only to trade with the Indians and convert the small number who would listen to the word of God.

The French also faced a number of other obstacles unfamiliar to most Spanish missionaries. There were relatively few Indians in the Northeast and Midwest, and the tribes in these regions were more sparsely settled and hostile to strangers, Indian and European. Long distances and frequent intertribal wars precipitated communications problems for the French and often forced them to choose sides. Adding to the confusion was the close proximity of English colonists who exacerbated the tribal wars to undermine alliances between the Indians and the French. All of these problems were compounded by the cold climate and the short growing season which limited the amount of travel and work that could be accomplished each year.

These obstacles seemed surmountable to men imbued with an extraordinary religious faith. French missionaries were among the first settlers in Canada at the beginning of the seventeenth century. At first, these priests ministered primarily to the Indians who lived in and around the French settlements. The establishment of the city of Quebec in 1608 led to the opening of vast territories to exploration and missionary work. Trading alliances with the Huron and Algonquin Indians eventually allowed missionaries to preach among these tribes.

Yet it would take twenty-five years for the French Church to send enough missionaries to make an impact on the Indians. It was not until the establishment of the Jesuit community in Quebec in 1632 that French missionary activity began in earnest. In fact, it would be the Jesuits who would dominate the French missions for the next 150 years.

Even though the Jesuits attempted to be systematic in their work, the conversion of the Indians was heavily dependent on the skills and commitment of few exceptional individuals. The self-sacrifice of priests such as Jean de Brebeuf, Gabriel Lelemant, Rene Menard, and Isaac Jogues was legendary. (*See Reading No. 2.*) These men literally devoted their lives to a valiant but vain effort to convert the Huron, the Algonquin, and even the savage Iroquois to Catholicism. Yet many Indians were fearful of Catholicism, thinking it something akin to witchcraft. "They say it causes them to die," wrote one Jesuit missionary, "and that it contains spells and charms which effect the destruction of their corn and engender contagious and general diseases wherewith the Iroquois now begin to be afflicted."

The stories of the exploits of these missionaries were quite remarkable and were regularly published in volumes known as *The Jesuit Relations*. "From these pages," notes historian William Bangert, "rises up vivid pictures of the cultivated and refined Black Robe squatting in a circle of filthy savages, or paddling his canoe across a wind-swept lake, or sleeping in a smoke-filled hut, or standing as an object of Indian derision.''*

From 1632 to 1649, Brebeuf and his colleagues established small but significant Christian communities among the Huron and Algonquin tribes, but these conversions came at a great price. The long-standing hostility between the Huron and the Iroquois put the missionaries in almost constant danger. Brebeuf, Lelemant, and Jogues, among others, all lost their lives at the hand of the Iroquois during the 1640s. Even though French civil authorities signed treaties with the Iroquois in the 1650s, the death of these Jesuit priests had a chilling effect on French missionary efforts. ''The difficult Huronia mission continued for fifteen years,'' notes James Hennesey, ''and they ended in an orgy of fire and death as the Iroquois unleashed a genocidal war on the Hurons in 1648–49. . . . Torture, mutilation, and running the gauntlet were only some of the features of these fiery days which saw ten thousand Hurons die and the remnant scattered.''†

This did not mean that the Jesuits abandoned the Indians. In fact, the martyrdom of Brebeuf and the others inspired a small band to expand their missionary work. By 1670 the Jesuits began a push into what is now central Canada and the midwestern United States. To facilitate this expansion, the order established a base of operations at St. Ignace on the Mackinac strait between the upper and lower peninsulas of Michigan. For the next century, St. Ignace would be the focal point for a Jesuit emphasis on exploration and conversion. In this new effort, success continued to be dependent on the abilities of a select number of extraordinary individuals.

There is little doubt that the Jesuits were among the greatest explorers of their time. They charted the rivers and terrain of what are now the states of Ohio, Michigan, Indiana, Illinois, Wisconsin, and Minnesota. The famous historian George Bancroft once wrote that ''not a cape was turned, nor a river

---

*William V. Bangert, *A History of the Society of Jesus* (St. Louis, 1972) p. 265.

†James Hennesey, *American Catholics: A History of the Roman Catholic Community in the United States* (New York, 1981) p. 25.

entered, but a Jesuit led the way.'' Although this is hyperbole, it is true that the Jesuits were among the first Europeans to explore vast expanses of the United States.

Certainly among the most famous of the explorer priests was the Jesuit Jacques Marquette, who was with the explorer Louis Jolliet in 1673 when he discovered the ''great river'' mentioned so often by the Indians. Within a month Jolliet and Marquette found the Mississippi and traveled as far south as the present state of Arkansas. They proved beyond doubt that the river ran north and south and that there were continuous waterways from the mouth of the St. Lawrence river in eastern Canada to the Mississippi Delta in the Gulf of Mexico.

Marquette's journey of discovery in the summer of 1673 was his one great voyage. He died two years later working among the Indians of Wisconsin. Although not noted at the time, Marquette's death also marked the beginning of the steady decline in French missionary work both in Canada and in the United States. The generation that had produced heroic priests such as Brebeuf, Jogues, and Marquette came to an end. The succeeding generations of Jesuits did not migrate to the New World in equivalent numbers, and those who did travel to Quebec worked among the Indians who had already converted to Catholicism. Gradually the missions declined to a low point in 1749 when only nineteen Jesuits remained in mission work in all of North America. This paltry number was cut even further by the French and Indian War (1754–1763) between France and England and the suppression of the Jesuit order by the Pope in 1763. By 1770, the French missionary presence in the United States was at an end.

CONCLUSION. The introduction and spread of Catholicism in the Western Hemisphere was an extraordinary experience, one aspect of a European quest for God, gold, and glory. With the discovery of a ''New World'' in the fifteenth century, a vast unexplored territory with millions of unbaptized souls opened up to the Church. How could both the riches of the land and the spiritual salvation of the Indians be secured for the greater glory of God? This was the challenge faced by the Spanish and French missionaries who traveled the North American continent.

Missionary work in the New World required exceptional faith and heroism. Indeed, the limited success of the Church in simultaneously exploring new territory and saving souls was due largely to the personal sacrifices and skills of a few great priests—Jogues, Marquette, Kino, and Serra, to name a few. Their willingness to give all, including their very lives, left a Catholic imprint on virtually every region of what is now the United States. A number of great American cities owe their existence to these French and Spanish priests.

The lasting impact of these missionaries was limited by the enormity of their task. In spite of the efforts of a few great men, the Church never had the resources or the ability to convert millions of Indians to Christ. By the end of the eighteenth century, the Spanish and French influence in America was in decline. In serving God and spurning gold, the missionaries earned glory, but personal sacrifice, faith, and heroism had not been enough for Catholicism to survive in America. The Church would need transplanted Catholics from Europe to establish a permanent foundation in America.

CHAPTER 3

COLONIAL CATHOLICISM, 1634–1789

While the Spanish and the French colonists actively promoted Catholicism, the British did all that they could to keep Catholicism out of their colonies. The suppression of Catholicism in England and its colonies stemmed from the divorce of King Henry VIII from his first wife, Catherine of Aragon, on May 23, 1533. Henry had appealed to Rome to annul his unhappy marriage, but the Pope refused. In response, an angry King Henry expelled the Catholic Church from England, seized Church property, and appointed himself head of a new religious denomination, the Church of England. English Catholics were pressured to abandon their faith and join the new Anglican Church.

When some Catholics resisted, English authorities became more vigilant and violent. Priests and bishops who were caught propagating Catholicism were expelled from England or in some cases hanged for their "crimes." Stories of Catholic subterfuge and intrigue abounded. Books such as John Foxe's *Book of Martyrs* (1563), tales of a 1605 plot by a Catholic named Guy Fawkes to blow up Parliament, and the 1678 "popish plot" to assassinate King Charles II were used to justify the suppression of English Catholicism.

What was policy and practice in the mother country was diligently enforced in the colonies. Virtually all the British-American colonial assemblies passed laws specifically proscribing the practice of Catholicism within their jurisdictions. It is not surprising, therefore, that few Catholics chose to emigrate to the British colonies, and those who did knew the meaning of persecution. Yet small Catholic communities of the faithful did manage to build firm foundations in several colonies despite the obstacles.

A FOUNDATION IN MARYLAND. The majority of the British Catholics who were brave enough to risk their lives on a perilous ocean voyage to the colonies chose Maryland as their destination. The colony had been founded in late 1633 through a royal charter given to Cecil Calvert, the second Lord Baltimore. Cecil's father, George Calvert, was a Catholic nobleman who had faithfully served the kings of England.

Eager to find a safe haven for fellow Catholics, the senior Calvert petitioned King Charles I for a charter to establish a New World colony for English Catholics. The colony was to lie north of Virginia and was to be named "Maryland," in honor of the late queen, Henriette Marie. The new colony was to have a large measure of religious freedom and Catholics would be openly allowed to practice their faith in Maryland, something they could not do in England at that time.

When the first colonists arrived on Maryland's shore in 1634, Catholics lived on equal terms with Protestants, a situation unique in the British colonies. Over the next fifteen years this denominational equality was codified by the Maryland assembly in several laws culminating in the "Act Concerning Religion" of 1649. Although badly flawed, especially in its lack of respect for non-Christian denominations, the Act was an important first step in the struggle for religious freedom in this country.

Within this tradition of limited religious freedom, Catholicism built a foundation with the Jesuits as the cornerstone. Led by Father Andrew White, the Jesuits worked among colonists and Indians alike who would listen to them preach. (*See Reading No. 5.*) To support themselves, the priests established a number of farms and became planters and traders as well as missionaries. It was these Jesuit priests, traveling to all parts of the colony as both ministers and businessmen, who gave the most visibility and identity to Catholicism during these early years.

Religious freedom did not last long in the colony. In 1654, a Puritan-dominated assembly repealed the 1649 toleration act and this led to attacks on Catholics. Some Catholic colonists were put to death, others were forced to flee. The Jesuit farms were plundered and the priests fled in disguise to Virginia. Although a measure of religious toleration was restored in 1660, the Catholic community in Maryland had received a bitter lesson on the fragile nature of their religious freedom. (*See Reading No. 6.*)

The Calvert family remained in control of the Maryland

colony until the "Glorious Revolution" of 1688 when a Protestant was restored to the British throne. Shortly thereafter,
the new king deposed the Catholic Calverts, made Maryland a
royal colony, and established the Anglican Church as the state
church of Maryland. All colonists, including Catholics, were
obliged to pay taxes to support it. This was only the first of
several new laws that were offensive to Maryland Catholics.
In later years, Catholics would be denied the vote, prohibited
from practicing their religion in public, and forbidden to establish schools for the instruction of their children.

Why did Catholics continue to live in a colony where they
were an unwanted and persecuted minority? In large part because the alternatives—moving to another colony or back to
England—would have been even worse. Though Maryland
failed to become the haven for Catholics promised by the Calverts, the colony was marginally more tolerant of Catholicism
than the mother country.

Maryland Catholics adjusted to the hostility of the Protestant majority by establishing insular communities. The typical
Catholic community was rural and consisted of twelve to
twenty families who lived within two miles of one another.
Their common bond was their religion, making Sundays and
holy days into social as well as religious occasions. Not surprisingly, Maryland Catholics trusted only one another; they
intermarried, became business partners, and collectively supported the Church. They frequently saw their priests outside of
church and invited them to participate in various social occasions. Religion was at the center of the life of every Maryland
Catholic during the seventeenth century.

It was also true that the practice of Catholicism in colonial
Maryland was a very private affair. No effort was made to
build Catholic churches or establish formal parishes. For the
most part, Maryland Catholics were discreet about the practice
of their faith. They feared the persecution and prejudice so
common in England. Those faithful close enough to one of the
Jesuit farms traveled there for Sunday Mass. The great Catholic plantation families built chapels adjoining their mansions
and recruited priests to staff them. Most other Catholics were
not so fortunate. Because of the general shortage of priests, a
large number of Catholic communities waited for traveling

Jesuit missionaries to celebrate Mass in one of the homes of the local Catholic farmers. Mass for these Catholics was a special occasion; on most Sundays these Catholics had to make do with their own services.

During the eighteenth century the Catholic communities in Maryland began to increase in size and visibility. Between 1700 and 1765, the number of Catholics in the colony increased from 2,500 to approximately 20,000, a rate of growth substantially greater than that of the general population. The reason for this growth can be traced in part to the large number of Irish immigrants arriving in Maryland during those years, a harbinger of future growth in the American Church. The increase in numbers led to a renewed if modest public presence for the Church. Separate church buildings were constructed for the first time in several decades and formal parishes were established. By the eve of the American Revolution in 1776, the Catholic Church had become an institution in Maryland.

CATHOLICISM IN OTHER COLONIES. Maryland was not an island. Small numbers of Catholics found their way to Virginia, Pennsylvania, and New York during the eighteenth century. The response to these Catholics was different in each colony. Except for Pennsylvania and Rhode Island, however, colonial Catholics found little but hostility in the British-American colonies.

As the colony adjoining Maryland, Virginia was a logical place to receive a few Catholic settlers. In fact, northern Virginia provided a haven for a number of Catholics during the anti-Catholic hostilities in Maryland in the 1650s. The Catholic families that journeyed across the Potomac river had hoped to find a more hospitable home than Maryland, but what they discovered was an anti-Catholic feeling that isolated and limited the growth of Virginia Catholicism. There were never more than a few Catholics in Virginia and all of them were in the northern part of the colony.

On a more tolerant note, Catholics were openly accepted in Pennsylvania. Chartered in 1681 by the Quaker William Penn, Pennsylvania committed itself to religious toleration in a manner only alluded to in Maryland. To be sure, there were several laws passed by the Pennsylvania general assembly in the eighteenth century that proscribed Catholics from full participation in colonial affairs, but there were no laws prohibiting Catholics from openly practicing their faith. It was a relative but real toleration that expectedly attracted Catholics to Penn's colony.

Those Catholics who chose Pennsylvania generally settled in the southeastern part of the colony. The largest congregation of Catholics lived in Philadelphia where the colony's first parish was established in 1734. Other Catholics—primarily German farmers from the Rhineland and the Palatinate—settled in the Susquehanna, Schuykill, and Delaware river valleys. These rural Catholics were served for many years by German priests who traveled the valleys on horseback.

New York was also home to a small Catholic community. The presence of Catholics in New York can be traced to James, Duke of York, namesake of the colony, brother of King Charles II, and later king of England himself. James became a Catholic in 1672 and two years later instructed the governor of his colony that religion should not be a criterion for settling in New York.

Catholics accepted the Duke's invitation to settle in New York. In fact, a number of Catholics held high office in the colony during the reign of King James II and the most prominent of these officials was Thomas Donegan who became governor of the colony in 1683. Donegan fostered religious liberty during his short term as governor and he welcomed Calvinists, Huguenots, and other dissenters to New York, but this religious toleration did not last. James was overthrown in the Glorious Revolution of 1688, and by 1700 Catholics were a persecuted minority in New York.

There were few Catholic communities in the other colonies, but anti-Catholicism flourished nonetheless. In fact, it seemed as if the harshest laws were passed by colonies that had never had a Catholic citizen. The very idea of tolerating the presence of Catholics was regarded as a sign of weakness in New England, a betrayal of English liberty and a denial of the righteousness of the Protestant faith. Isolation, the lack of any contact with Catholics, and stories of English Catholic plots and conspiracies all intensified the anti-Catholicism in those northern colonies.

THE AMERICAN REVOLUTION. The American Revolution brought about a change in the status of Catholics in the former British colonies. The religious restrictions of the colonial era were swept aside as a large segment of colonial society—Catholic and non-Catholic—united to fight England. Protestants may not have liked Catholics, but for the sake of independence, they were willing to tolerate the "Papists." Protestant editors and clergymen turned their pens away from the "evils" of Catholicism to any and all who gave comfort to the detested "redcoats."

More important, the laws which kept Catholics from full citizenship in the colonies were not included in the new state constitutions of the 1770s. Many states, moreover, took the initiative of incorporating into their constitutions sections or statutes on the freedom of conscience and religion. Pennsylvania was among the first states to respond by passing a new constitution in September, 1776. Maryland followed in November with a constitution that lifted all restrictions on the practice of Catholicism and on Catholics themselves.

What accounts for this significant shift in attitude toward Catholics and Catholicism? There are several factors involved, not the least of which was the military assistance provided by Catholic France to the rebellious colonies. The rebels could ill afford to offend their allies during a war for independence. A second fact was leadership. Men like George Washington and Thomas Jefferson detested bigotry of any kind; they took every opportunity to attack religious prejudice in colonial society. If the colonies were to be a new nation based on the principle that all men are created equal, religious prejudice generally and anti-Catholicism specifically would have to be eliminated.

The Catholic community responded enthusiastically to the call for revolution and this commitment was symbolized in the contributions of Charles Carroll of Carrollton. A member of one of Maryland's wealthiest families, Carroll was as committed to liberty as he was to his religious faith. Writing in 1773 under the pen name "First Citizen," Carroll exposed the arbitrary rule of Maryland's governor in a series of newspaper debates with a loyalist named "Antillon." Carroll's arguments were an important factor in swinging the assembly elections that year in favor of the patriots. (*See Reading No. 7.*) Along with John Rutledge, Carroll was one of the two Catholics to sign the Declaration of Independence.

Other Catholics also responded to the call for patriots. Daniel Carroll joined his cousin Charles as a member of the Continental Congress. Another Catholic, Thomas Fitzsimons, served as a delegate from Pennsylvania. Catholics also fought and died for their new country. With Captain John Barry at sea and General Stephan Moylan in the field, the patriotism of colonial Catholics was beyond reproach.

With the end of the war in 1783, the challenge facing Catholics in the postwar years was to build a national church. Now that they were free to practice their faith without fear of punishment, what sort of denomination would Catholics establish? Who would lead the Church in the United States? What sort of schools, hospitals, asylums, and seminaries would be needed? The Vatican responded by leaving these matters in the hands of yet another member of the Carroll family. In 1784, Father John Carroll, brother of Daniel and cousin of Charles, was named by the Pope as superior of the American Catholic missions.

Carroll believed that the American Revolution had created "a blessing and an advantage" for American Catholics. Catholics in this new nation were free of all foreign domination; no longer were they "colonials," they were "Americans." To symbolize and solidify this identity within the Catholic community, Carroll petitioned the Pope to appoint an *American* bishop. The Church in this new nation needed organization and leadership.

Yet Carroll knew that the appointment of an American bishop would not resolve the major problem facing his denomination in America—a drastic shortage of priests. Since 1634, priests for America had come from Europe and this process was sufficient to meet the needs of a small, somewhat persecuted religion. But freedom brought a renewed interest in Catholicism and the formation of many new parishes scattered around the country. European seminaries found it difficult to meet the demand for priests in America.

To nurture a native priesthood, Carroll proposed the establishment of a national Catholic academy and seminary in the United States. Carroll was well aware that it would take many years to fulfill his dream of an American priesthood. In the meantime, Carroll was prepared to accept an alternative plan in which the laity would take a greater role.

The trustee movement, as it later was called, encouraged the laity to take over the temporal affairs of the parishes. Many Catholic communities elected leadership committees, collected funds, purchased land, constructed church buildings, and provided for their maintenance. It was a democratic system of church government in tune with the egalitarian spirit of the new country. In fact, the trustee movement gave Catholicism in the United States a decidedly American identity for the next two generations.

The lack of national leadership, the shortage of priests, and the importance of lay participation were the hallmarks of the Catholic Church in the United States in the 1780s. (*See Reading No. 8.*) The American Church was the oldest denomination seeking an identity in the newest nation in the world. Over the next century the American Church would grow and expand in the numbers of dioceses, priests, and communicants. But each generation would struggle with a question first posed in the 1780s—what is the proper relationship between Catholicism and democracy?

CONCLUSION. The practice of Catholicism in the British-American colonies was a survival story. For the most part, Catholics were an unwanted, even detested, minority in seventeenth and eighteenth century America. Only Pennsylvania consistently showed much toleration for those colonists who professed spiritual loyalty to the Pope at Rome. Even Maryland, originally founded as a haven for Catholics, soon fell to persecuting them.

This is not to say that Catholicism did not have an impact on the colonies. Certainly the tradition of religious toleration, first introduced in the colonies by the Catholics of Maryland, has been of lasting importance in American life. In a less visible but no less important way, thousands of Catholic settlers contributed to the material well-being and later political survival of the colonies as they were forged into a new nation.

Unlike the Spanish and French colonies, where the survival and success of Catholicism was due to a few great priests, Catholicism in the British colonies had a broader base of support. There is no question that the Jesuit order was primarily responsible for keeping the Catholic tradition alive in the British-American colonies in the seventeenth century. The work of these priests was supported and enhanced by a growing population of transplanted English Catholics. The extended network of Catholic families—the Brents, the Neales, and the Carrolls, for example—was evidence that Catholicism could survive if not exactly prosper in the New World.

By the end of the eighteenth century, when Catholicism was in decline in the Spanish and French colonies, the Catholics of the British-American colonies had earned the right to practice their religion openly. No longer outcasts concerned primarily with survival, these recently independent Catholics faced a new challenge—how to shape a national denomination out of an increasingly diverse population of transplanted European Catholics with divergent loyalties. It was a challenge that would face the American Church and its leaders for more than a century.

CHAPTER 4

CATHOLICISM IN A YOUNG REPUBLIC, 1789–1829

Two important events took place in 1789 that profoundly affected the course of American Catholicism for the next two centuries. In April, the first federal congress convened and George Washington became the first President of the United States under the recently ratified Constitution. It was a government with checks and balances, one that would soon codify religious liberty as one of the principles of a Bill of Rights. Another less noticed event took place on November 16, when the Vatican appointed John Carroll to become the first Catholic bishop in the United States. (*See Reading No. 9.*) It was the Vatican's recognition that Catholicism was no longer a persecuted denomination in the United States.

Carroll had not sought the leadership of the Catholic Church in America, but he accepted the position with a spirit of commitment. It was most important, he believed, that an *American* be appointed the first bishop. If he refused the appointment, Rome might well send a foreigner to serve as the first bishop. Thus Carroll assumed responsibility for a national diocese based at Baltimore that included about 35,000 Catholics, most of whom lived in Maryland and Pennsylvania with small communities emerging in Massachusetts, New York, and Kentucky.

Even though there was a significant number of prominent Catholic families in the United States, most American Catholics at the end of the eighteenth century were poor farmers. They were simple people who were faithful to their religion but lacked "the fervor which is developed by constant exhortations to piety." Compounding this problem was the annual arrival of tens of thousands of Catholic immigrants from Ireland and Germany, many of whom were completely ignorant of their Faith. Carroll's task was to shape this motley collection of lay people into an American Church loyal to Rome.

ORGANIZING THE AMERICAN CHURCH. As the first step in organizing his denomination, Carroll committed himself and his meager resources to the establishment of schools for the education of future clergy and lay leaders. Carroll vigorously worked for the establishment of ''Georgetown Academy'' (later University) in 1789 and called upon his flock to support the new institution. The new bishop was well aware that one academy could not possibly suffice for the growing number of American Catholics, but he argued that Georgetown would mold lay leaders who would return home and educate other Catholics both by word and by example.

Behind Carroll's call for the laity to support Georgetown was the more important hope that the school would foster a significant increase in religious vocations. He also knew that cultivating vocations was only half the battle; he needed to provide formal training for young Americans entering the priesthood. Carroll was skeptical that a seminary could succeed in America because there were few potential clerical students in the country, but he was open minded. When, in the aftermath of the French Revolution, a group of Sulpician priests arrived in the United States, Carroll permitted them to establish a seminary if they also would do missionary work. In July 1791, the bishop's skepticism gave way with the opening of St. Mary's Seminary. ''All our hopes are founded on the Seminary of Baltimore,'' he wrote to the Pope a year later.

There was sheer frustration in Carroll's effort to cultivate a native clergy. For all his work, the majority of the newly ordained priests in the United States during Carroll's tenure as bishop were foreign born and foreign educated. It was not until 1799 that Carroll had the satisfaction of ordaining the first American-born priest. Even though the number of American-educated priests increased during Carroll's tenure, he worried about the origins and loyalties of his largely foreign clergy.

Yet Carroll had no choice but to accept them. Like many American bishops who would follow him, Carroll was forced to accept foreign-born priests to meet the critical needs of his parishes. What the bishop learned after the fact was that such large numbers of foreigners precipitated the major crisis of early American Catholicism.

Most foreign-born priests had a deep commitment to the European ideal of Catholicism. In Europe, bishops and priests, kings and nobles decided the affairs of church and state; the common man was expected to obey both civic and religious edicts without question. Although Americans, including American Catholics, had been deciding their own affairs for more than a century, it was inevitable that priests and people would clash over the question of leadership in the American Church in the first years of the nineteenth century.

The battleground during these years was, of course, the parish. It was Church practice that bishops and their priests had the right to control Catholic parishes, but tradition did not mean much to Catholics who had pooled their funds to build churches and schools and hired teachers to educate their children. The laity saw no reason to consult with the bishop or even the local priest about the temporal affairs of their parishes. In fact, many parishioners expected the bishop to consult them about the appointment of pastors.

During the years 1789 to 1829, the laity in Virginia, South Carolina, Pennsylvania, and New York fought with their bishops and their pastors over temporal parish affairs. The reasons for these extended struggles varied from parish to parish. In Philadelphia, for example, a local layman named James Oellers convinced his fellow parishioners at Holy Trinity Church to follow him rather than obey their parish priest. The largely German parishioners had wanted a German pastor and Oellers had exploited their discontent. For nearly twenty years Oellers battled with Bishop Carroll. "He has managed all of the affairs of Holy Trinity Church, both sacred and otherwise, to suit his own fancy," wrote Carroll in frustration. "Trusteeism," as it was called, proved to be the most significant internal conflict in American Catholicism in the years before the Civil War.

AMERICAN CATHOLIC SOCIETY. Even though lay-clerical conflicts and shortages of priests were major problems, they did not seem to limit the growth of American Catholicism. The arrival of increasing numbers of Irish and German Catholic immigrants in Boston, New York, and Philadelphia underscored the need for more dioceses. Finally in 1808, Baltimore was raised to the level of archdiocese and new dioceses were established at Boston, New York, Philadelphia, and at Bardstown in frontier Kentucky. In something of an autocratic fashion, Carroll nominated candidates for bishops of these new dioceses without consulting either priests or laity.

The early histories of these dioceses reflect different problems and conflicts. In Boston, for example, the promise of rapid growth in the Catholic community did not materialize. In 1820, the Boston diocese, which covered all of New England in those early years, had only 3,500 Catholics and 750 of those were Indians in Maine. In fact, the Boston diocese was so small that it was twice suggested that the diocese be merged with New York.

The small number of Catholics in Boston and the charm and diplomacy of the first bishop—Jean Cheverus—minimized the conflicts that plagued the Church elsewhere in America. Relations between Bishop Cheverus and the greater Boston community were extraordinary. The first Catholic cathedral was designed by the noted Federalist architect Charles Bulfinch and among the contributors to the building fund were John Adams and John Quincy Adams, Harrison Grey Otis, and other prominent non-Catholics. When Cheverus was transferred back to France in 1823, the city protested.

When Benedict Fenwick succeeded Cheverus, Irish immigration began to swell, making the non-Catholic population uneasy, and threatened the good feeling that had prevailed. These new Catholics had none of the sophistication of Bishop Cheverus, and the non-Catholic population feared that this immigrant rabble would breed disease and crime. This uneasiness and concern would later manifest itself in anti-Catholicism in Massachusetts throughout the 1830s.

The situation in New York was bad almost from the start. Catholics in New York struggled to provide for the spiritual and temporal needs of a deluge of new Catholics who arrived in the years from 1800 to 1830. At the turn of the century, the Catholic community in New York had found it difficult to sustain even a single parish. (*See Reading No. 10.*) Within a decade this parish was overwhelmed; the number of Catholics in New York jumped from about 1,300 in 1800 to almost 15,000 a decade later.

Adding to Catholic New York's problems was a lack of leadership. Even though New York was made a diocese in

1808, a resident bishop did not arrive until 1815. Bishop John Connolly arrived in that year to find about 15,000 Catholics, four priests and two parishes. Connolly struggled to improve these statistics and recruited eighteen priests for the new diocese before he died in 1825. Connolly was succeeded by the saintly but ineffective John DuBois, who would weather the same of kind of anti-Catholic hostility in the 1830s that faced Bishop Fenwick in Boston.

The bishops of Boston and New York had troubled but somewhat productive tenures during the first third of the nineteenth century, not so the first two bishops of Philadelphia. The tenures of Michael Egan and Henry Conwell were unmitigated disasters. It was ironic that the so-called "city of brotherly love," would be the setting for an acrimonious battle of extraordinary proportions between Philadelphia's bishops, priests, and laity.

Bishop Egan was a saintly man, but a poor administrator. During his four years in Philadelphia, he waged a constant battle for control of St. Mary's Church, the city's principal parish. The hardship and the heartache of this conflict led to his early death in 1814. Egan was not replaced for six years and during this time the situation in Philadelphia rapidly deteriorated. Each parish was left to its own devices. After three other men had refused the appointment, the bishopric of Philadelphia fell to Henry Conwell, an elderly Irish priest, who did no better than Egan in administering the diocese. Constant fighting led to chaos before order was restored. Catholicism in Philadelphia had become a national scandal by the 1820s.

The new diocese of Bardstown shared some of the experiences of the eastern dioceses, but frontier Catholicism also had some unique features worth noting. Catholicism had come to Kentucky in the 1780s when Marylanders migrated into the future state in search of more fertile land. By 1815 there were a reported 10,000 Catholics in Kentucky with the majority in or near the settlement of Bardstown in the central part of the state.

Tension developed within the Kentucky community over the issue of local leadership. The lay Catholics who had established the parishes and built the churches were native-born, independent frontiersmen; they expected to share in the leadership of their Church. The new bishop and priests in the state were French for the most part; they remembered the excesses of the French Revolution and were suspicious of a laity that claimed "the extravagant excesses of Republicanism" in the governance of local Church affairs. The tension between the clergy and the laity festered in the 1820s and later resulted in the type of conflict found in Philadelphia.

Although relations between Catholic bishops and their flocks were chaotic during these years, it also was true that many Catholics were successful in establishing social institutions that would later bring order to American Catholicism. The first Catholic hospitals, schools, asylums, and colleges were established during the years from 1789 to 1829 and these institutions provided much needed support to the growing Catholic community.

Another institution that brought a measure of order and unity to the American Church was the *United States Catholic Miscellany,* the first American Catholic weekly newspaper. Established in 1822 by Bishop John England of Charleston, the *Miscellany* provided an important communications link among Catholics in different dioceses and encouraged a greater unity of purpose among Catholics on the national level. Not surprisingly, the *Miscellany* became the model for the dozens of diocesan Catholic newspapers established over the next generation.

CATHOLIC WOMEN RELIGIOUS. No group contributed more to bringing order and structure to American Catholicism in these early years than the first communities of women religious. During the years from 1789 to 1829, eight such communities were established in the United States: the Carmelites in 1790, the Visitation Sisters in 1799, the Daughters of Charity in 1809, the Sisters of Loretto in 1812, the Sisters of Charity of Nazareth also in 1812, the Dominican Sisters in 1822, the Oblate Sister of Providence in 1829, and the Sisters of Charity of Our Lady of Mercy also in 1829. These "highly respectable and accomplished ladies," as one contemporary newspaper called the sisters, established many of the social institutions that would give an organizational structure to Catholicism throughout the nineteenth century.

Who were these courageous young women? Research by historian Barbara Misner* shows that most of the novices entering American Catholic religious orders during these years were American-born women of middle class backgrounds. It was a distinct contrast to the foreign origins of most American priests. On the surface, Misner notes, these young women appeared to be like other American women of the same era. Yet, it is also true that these women religious had a commitment to service that was not typical of other young women. Through the religious life, a young Catholic woman could make an important contribution to both her Church and her nation.

The spirit of service filled Elizabeth Seton and the religious congregation that she founded in 1809. It was Seton's vision of an order of teaching sisters, and the subsequent establishment of the Daughters of Charity at Emmitsburg, Maryland, which became the framework for the growth of American Catholic schooling during the early decades of the nineteenth century.

During her short tenure as mother superior of the order, Seton responded to numerous requests to establish schools and asylums in various Catholic communities. Staffing fifteen schools in eleven cities in the years from 1809 to 1830, the Daughters of Charity brought a measure of stability and order to an often chaotic denomination. It is for this reason that Elizabeth Seton acquired the reputation of being the ''foundress'' of the American Catholic parochial school system.

Seton was a model for many other committed women who established religious communities in the United States during the next century. These women religious faced extraordinary hardships and yet succeeded in building and sustaining an impressive network of schools, hospitals, and asylums in major American cities across the country. In many of these cities, these social institutions made important contributions to im-

---

*Barbara Misner, ''A Comparative Study of the Members and Apostolates of the First Eight Permanent Communities of Women Religious within the Original Borders of the United States, 1790–1850,'' Ph.D. dissertation, Catholic University of America, 1980.

proving the quality of urban life. Catholic women religious did more to foster and sustain American Catholicism than any other group within the Church.

NATIONAL CHURCH LEADERSHIP. In spite of the significant contributions of women religious and other dedicated Catholics, disorder remained the hallmark of American Catholicism throughout the 1810s and 1820s. Contests between bishops, priests, and laity raged in a number of dioceses. (*See Reading No. 11.*) As if to make matters worse, the continuing arrival of millions of Catholic immigrants from Europe increased the size, diversity, and confusion within the American Catholic community.

Bishop John England of Charleston argued for a council of all the American bishops to address common problems and speak with one voice to the growing Catholic community. "The deranged and unsettled state of the American Church," he wrote, "can be reduced to order and peace and permanent system only by Provincial Synods of the American Hierarchy." But few of his fellow bishops agreed with England's assessment of the need for synods; most preferred to address Church problems as if they were purely local in nature. Finally in 1829, England got his wish—the First Provincial Council of Baltimore was held that October.

The council issued no radical proposals for changes in Church structure, liturgy, or discipline. The bishops contented themselves with pastoral letters to the laity that emphasized the need for more priests and reminded parents about the importance of providing religious education for their children. (*See Reading No.12.*) Yet the First Provincial Council of Baltimore was important because it established a tradition of collegiality and national leadership among the American bishops. Over the next forty-five years, the bishops met nine more times at Baltimore to discuss Church affairs and to prepare pastoral letters on the state of American Catholicism. These councils and their resulting pastoral letters charted the course of Catholicism during the middle years of the nineteenth century.

CONCLUSION. The forty years after John Carroll was appointed the first Bishop of Baltimore were a time of chaos in American Catholicism. These decades were marked by frequent conflicts over the control of local parishes; rapid and sustained growth through immigration; a growing need for more churches, schools, and priests; and a general confusion over the direction of the Church in the United States.

Some order did emerge out of the chaos; the issues that dominated the American Church in the years from 1789 to 1829 would shape Catholicism for the next century. Conflicts between the laity and the clergy would occur repeatedly in the nineteenth century. Immigration, and the decidedly foreign influence of these new Catholics, shaped the identity of the Church well into the twentieth century. The constant need for more social institutions—schools, hospitals, asylums—preoccupied all of the bishops who followed John Carroll. Finally, the First Plenary Council of Baltimore established a collegial tradition within the American Catholic hierarchy that continued to 1884 and that reemerged after 1919. In these many ways the years 1789 to 1829 were the formative years of American Catholicism.

CHAPTER 5

AN IMMIGRANT CHURCH, 1830–1885

American Catholicism experienced rapid and constant change during the middle years of the nineteenth century. A tremendous influx of immigrants transformed American Catholicism from a small minority denomination into the largest church in the country and the once native-born denomination became overwhelmingly foreign-born. Such dramatic demographic shifts precipitated a series of challenges and crises not only for Catholic leaders, but also for native Americans. Could these impoverished foreigners become patriotic, productive Americans and still remain loyal to their Church? There was more than one way to respond to this question.

Catholic leaders were overwhelmed by the challenge of providing for the spiritual welfare of such a diverse flock. In fact, the Church establishment lacked the resources to meet the needs of the native Catholic congregations let alone respond to the more significant needs of these new arrivals. These leaders were well aware that they would have to find more priests to administer the sacraments and find more nuns to tend the sick, care for the orphans, and teach the children. They would have to raise funds to build new churches, hospitals, orphanages, and schools. Even though the Catholic bishops of the United States wanted to establish a self-reliant American Church, they had no choice but to look to Europe for the necessary resources.

AMERICAN CATHOLIC SOCIETY. What had caused millions of Catholics to abandon their native lands for the United States? In fact, there were dozens of reasons why the peasants of Europe came to the New World. Simple economics was a major factor. The population of Europe had doubled between 1750 and 1815, putting a strain on the food supply. The introduction of large-scale farming and the rise of the factory system had displaced millions of peasants and forced them to find new sources of livelihood. The most significant causes of emigration were the monumental catastrophes that struck both Ireland and Germany in the 1840s.

Between 1846 and 1851, Ireland suffered a famine that dec-
imated its population and forced millions of Irish men and
women to flee their native land. Poor, impoverished Ireland
had relied for generations on the potato to provide sustenance
for her people. A family of six, for example, could live for a
year on the potato harvest of little more than an acre of land.
Unfortunately, the potato was prone to disease and in 1846 the
worst blight in history struck the land. Famine weakened the
the population, lowering resistance to all forms of disease.
Typhus and "relapsing fever" were epidemic across the Em-
erald Isle. It is difficult to determine the fate of Ireland's population; at least a million people died between 1846 and 1851
and another 1.5 million emigrated, many of them to the
United States.

German Catholics also suffered through a number of economic shocks that squeezed both farmers and artisans. For
centuries, Catholic peasants had bartered with landowners for
the use of farm land. By the middle of the nineteenth century,
these property owners were demanding cash instead of produce. Peasants found themselves constantly in need of cash;
tens of thousand of tenant farmers were forced off the land
because they failed to raise sufficient cash. In the cities German Catholic artisans also faced increased competition in the
manufacture of finished goods; many lost their jobs to im-
ports. There were other reasons for the German Catholic exodus—incidents of religious and political persecution in the
1840s, for example—but economics was the principal reason
for emigration in the years 1830 to 1885.

Why did they come to America, a Protestant nation? Quite
simply these immigrants were invited. Handbills and cheap
newspapers from the United States circulated in every country
in Europe, inviting and encouraging emigration. These publications were printed and distributed by American entrepre-
neurs seeking a new source of labor for a rapidly expanding
economy. If Europe did not need or want these peasants,
America would make them into factory workers, railroad laborers, hod carriers, and farm hands.

The Irish became city dwellers for the most part. Although
they had been farmers in Ireland, the land had failed them; the
Irish took jobs where they could find them and these jobs were

in urban areas. By 1850, cities such as Boston, New York, Philadelphia, and Baltimore reported sizable Irish communities—as much as one quarter of the total populations. As the railroads moved west to the cities of Buffalo, Cleveland, Detroit, Chicago, and Milwaukee, so also did the Irish. Indeed, they helped to build the railroads that connected these cities with the East. New waves of Irish immigrants joined their relatives in the cities of the Northeast and Midwest, making these the regions of choice for the Irish for the next century.

The Germans pursued a distinctly different course. To be sure, many German Catholics chose to live in the same cities as the Irish. Most Germans—Catholics included—were farmers in their homeland and they were determined to be farmers in America. By 1850, approximately half of the Germans who emigrated to this country had settled in the so-called "German Triangle"—the region roughly bordered by the cities of Cincinnati, St. Louis, and Milwaukee.

A hearty band of independent minded immigrants followed no pattern at all. Some Irishmen ventured west and south, providing cities such as San Francisco and New Orleans with sizable immigrant populations. The Germans pushed farther west and south into Iowa, Minnesota, and even Texas. By 1885, the Catholic population was spread across the country in an uneven distribution.

As the Catholic population grew, the need for more dioceses was self-evident and their establishment followed the pattern of settlement. Detroit became a diocese in 1833, followed by Vincennes, Indiana in 1834, and Nashville, Tennessee in 1837. Chicago and Milwaukee were both made dioceses in 1843, and others soon followed. By the time of the First Plenary of Baltimore in 1852, there were six archdioceses, twenty-five dioceses, and more than 2,100 churches and mission stations in the new nation. Over the next half-century, the continued growth and expansion of the Catholic population would lead to the establishment of an additional fifty-five dioceses, eighty percent of which were in the Northeast or Midwest.

For the majority of these immigrant Catholics, the concept of diocese meant little because the parish was the focal point of their religion. As different immigrant groups settled in various dioceses, they built churches and petitioned local bishops for pastors of their own nationality. Not surprisingly, these parishes had a distinctly European style, an effort to preserve the village Catholicism of the homeland.

The organization of the "national" parish was pioneered by the Germans who believed that native languages and culture were needed to preserve the faith. (*See Reading No. 14.*) National parishes allowed the Germans and later the Poles, the Italians, and other ethnic groups to preserve part of their past in a new and frustrating world. The national parish also insured that the next generation would be raised understanding the language and the culture of their forebears. The national parish was an important if divisive element within American Catholicism for the next century.

Any portrait of the American Catholic Church during the middle years of the nineteenth century would show a denomination of loosely affiliated dioceses with loosely affiliated parishes administered by priests who had little in common with one another except their foreign origins and their commitment to Catholicism. Each ethnic group was an island unto itself with little communication among different groups. In fact, the distinctly foreign and parish based loyalties of most of these new Catholics precipitated leadership crises in many dioceses.

NATIONAL CHURCH LEADERSHIP. Who would lead the American Church was still an open question in 1830. To be sure, the Vatican had selected bishops to serve as leaders of each diocese, but the will of the Vatican was not enough to merit the respect of many American Catholics. American bishops in the nineteenth century faced a set of circumstances that challenged even the best of the lot. Disobedient priests, rebellious laymen, and interethnic rivalries made it difficult for the men selected by Rome to lead their flocks. More than one American priest turned away from the Holy Father's call, dreading the problems of diocesan leadership. More than one bishop was institutionalized or retired prematurely due to the tensions of American Catholic leadership.

To a significant extent these nineteenth-century bishops mirrored the ethnic and social composition of the Catholic population. Only about one-third of the bishops appointed during these years were native-born; most bishops were either Irish or French with a scattering from Austria, Belgium, Canada, Switzerland, and Germany. As a group they were collegial, meeting in council ten times in the years from 1829 to 1884. At each of these councils the bishops attempted to use moral suasion, praise, and guilt to direct American Catholics in the ways of the Faith. In the final analysis, however, it was up to individual bishops to address the problems within their own dioceses.

In an effort to discuss common problems, learn from one another, and speak with a common voice, the bishops met periodically in councils. Ten provincial and three plenary (national) councils were held in Baltimore between 1829 and 1884. These meetings provided opportunities for older, more experienced bishops to advise their less experienced colleagues. The importance of these meetings was to establish firmly a collegial tradition in national Church leadership; since John Carroll's time, national Catholic leadership has been symbolized in the gatherings of the nation's bishops in council.

The interludes between council meetings varied significantly. The first seven meetings were provincial councils that were held approximately every three years as was Church tradition. Although the number of Catholics in the United States had grown substantially in the first half of the century, the Church continued to be one vast archdiocese with an archbishop at Baltimore. Every three years between 1829 and 1849 the Catholic bishops of the United States traveled to Baltimore to discuss the state of Catholicism. The major result of these councils was a national sense of unity and purpose.

The bishops met in council three more times in the nineteenth century, in 1852, 1866, and 1884. As was the tradition, they continued to meet in Baltimore. These later assemblies were called plenary councils, meaning that they brought together bishops from several archdioceses. The 1852 meeting, for example, drew 32 archbishops and bishops who represented more than 1.5 million Catholics and over 1,500 priests. Although not known for its legislation, the 1852 council was important because it underscored the growth and strength of the Church in America. By 1850, Catholicism was the largest single Christian denomination in the United States.

The Second Plenary Council was held in 1866, shortly after the Civil War, at a time when most Protestant denominations were divided between north and south. The council was attended by 45 archibishops, bishops and abbots representing four million Catholics and over 3,000 priests. The stated purpose of the meeting was to standardize Church procedure and to remind the laity of the centrality of episcopal authority; the unstated purpose was to emphasize that American Catholicism could rise above regional differences to sustain itself as a national denomination.

The language of the letter they issued emphasized the importance of the bishops as leaders. "Bishops, therefore, who are successors of the apostles," noted the 1866 pastoral letter, "are inspired from on high with the gift of inerrancy, so that the body or college can never fail or define anything against doctrine revealed by God." There was no question as to who would lead the Church in America.

The Third Plenary Council of 1884 further consolidated the authority of the bishops over their flocks. Meeting for four weeks at the end of that year, 72 archbishops and bishops codified liturgical and ecclesial practice in the United States. More important, the bishops addressed an entire panoply of social issues, each time providing specific guidance to the laity. They cautioned the laity to observe the Lord's Day by abstaining from work and liquor and by attending Mass.

The bishops also wrestled with the question of labor unions and secret societies. Many of the more liberal bishops were favorably disposed toward these organizations, noting that unions did much to protect the workingmen. The conservatives, however, were deeply suspicious of these groups and moved to have all such organizations condemned. The end result was a condemnation of secret societies, but no recommendation against labor unions. The Catholic Church would gain the reputation as a defender of the workingman.

Yet of all the issues addressed by the Third Plenary Council, educational matters were its greatest contribution. The bishops authorized the compilation of a national catechism and the establishment of a national Catholic university. Of primary importance, was that they instructed the laity to support parochial schools. "All Catholic parents are to send their children to the parish school," noted the decree, "unless it is evident that a sufficient training in religion is given either in the homes or in other Catholic schools." Those parishes without schools were to build schools within two years. Unquestionably, education was the single most significant priority of the bishops at the Third Plenary Council.

The bishops saw the need to provide more continuity in the leadership of national Church affairs than that provided by periodic councils. Accordingly the bishops approved the establishment of a committee of archbishops to meet annually to address national Church issues. The mantle of leadership passed from all of the bishops assembled in council to a smaller group; for the next thirty-five years, this committee of archbishops would wrestle with an unprecedented variety of complex problems facing American Catholicism.

National Church affairs did not have much of an impact on leadership achieved by a bishop in his own diocese. The circumstances faced by each bishop varied from diocese to diocese, making it difficult to generalize about the dynamics of diocesan leadership. However, one common challenge faced by all of these men was episcopal authority. (*See Reading No. 15.*) From the time of the foundation of the American Church, lay people had exerted substantial authority over local Church affairs and they continued to do so during the years of massive immigration. Lay Catholics—particularly the Germans—would buy land, build churches, and petition local bishops for the appointment of pastors. Often these immigrants retained title to Church property, unwilling to surrender their control to the bishops.

Gradually the laity gave way to episcopal authority. By the last quarter of the nineteenth century, lay involvement in Church affairs was largely advisory. The pastors, firm allies of the local bishop were in control in most parishes. The laity was left "to pay, pray and obey." This is not to say that the question of who would lead the Church was completely resolved by 1885. Indeed, there were conflicts between local pastors and bishops during the last quarter of the nineteenth century and various ethnic communities continued to protest the dominance of Irish bishops. But by 1885, control of Church property and the appointment of pastors were firmly in the hands of the American bishops. They would further consolidate that authority in the first quarter of the twentieth century.

CATHOLIC-PROTESTANT CONFLICT. The annual arrival of millions of foreigners was the cause of tension between Catholics and Protestants. Native-born Protestants worried about the loyalties of these new arrivals. Would Catholic immigrants ever become fully American? (*See Reading No. 13.*) American Protestants vowed to do all in their power to exert influence over these unruly foreigners but, unfortunately, this influence often came in the form of violence. The middle years of the nineteenth century were marked with dozens of anti-Catholic riots and other violent confrontations. Religion was a very divisive issue during these years.

Attacks against Catholic churches, priests, nuns, and the laity occurred in most major cities during the years before the Civil War. Boston, New York, Philadelphia, Baltimore, Cincinnati, Louisville, Detroit, St. Louis—all were settings for violent street fighting between Catholics and Protestants. Two confrontations stand out as important case studies of anti-Catholicism: the burning of the Ursuline Convent near Boston in 1834 and the Philadelphia Bible Riots of 1844. The repercussions of these and other anti-Catholic incidents lasted for two generations.

From the time of their arrival in Boston in 1818, the Ursuline Sisters had operated a convent school for Congregational and Unitarian as well as Catholic girls. Fearful of any collusion between Unitarians and Catholics, Congregational ministers began to attack the convent school from their pulpits in the early 1830s. Tension in the neighborhoods near the convent increased as the rhetorical attacks became more numerous and vociferous in the early months of 1834. The nervous breakdown and ''escape'' of one of the Ursuline Sisters in July precipitated rumors about the barbarity and immorality of the convent. Finally on August 11, a mob of workingmen torched the convent and an adjoining farmhouse. There was little remorse among Boston Protestants. The trial of the arsonists was a farce as the accused were not only exonerated, but also applauded as heros. Boston Catholics turned inward, alienated from the hostile world around them.

The emergence of organized anti-Catholicism in Philadelphia, in the form of nativist "American-Republican" clubs, led to the worst anti-Catholic rioting in American history. Campaigning in the municipal elections in May 1844, the American-Republicans held a rally on the edge of one of the city's Irish neighborhoods. Fighting broke out between nativists and Catholics and a young Protestant boy was killed in the melee. The north side of the city quickly became a battleground; Catholic homes were set on fire, a Catholic church and parsonage were burned, and thousands were left homeless. Order was not restored in Philadelphia for three days and the tension never subsided. Renewed fighting broke out in early July when a second Catholic church was attacked and destroyed. The riots of 1844 left the Philadelphia Catholic community embittered for many years.

The violence and confrontation of the early part of the 1840s gave way to a relative calm in the later years of the decade and continued into the 1850s. Even the war with Catholic Mexico did not precipitate any more physical attacks on American Catholics. The war of words never abated; by one estimate more than 2.2 million pages of anti-Catholic literature appeared in 1849 alone. Protestants regularly attacked Catholics in the pages of their denominational newspapers and were rebutted the next week in the Catholic press. Catholics would publish inflammatory tirades against the injustice of the common school and the denominational papers would respond with a stirring defense. Nothing but bitterness resulted from these "debates." The end result was the emergence of social barriers between Catholics and Protestants that would last for more than a century.

REBELLION AND REUNIFICATION. Certainly the greatest tragedy faced by American Catholicism during these years was the Civil War. Just as Northerner fought Southerner, so also did Catholic fight Catholic. In spite of all the divisiveness caused by the war, there never was any hint that this conflict would divide American Catholicism permanently as it

divided other denominations. Little more than a year after the
end of the war, all the Catholic bishops of the United States,
both North and South, met in plenary council. This national
meeting was a symbol of the fundamental unity within American Catholicism.

The war itself was fought to preserve the union, but the
southern states had rebelled, in part, because of restrictions on
the ownership of slaves. Slave labor had always been a fundamental part of southern life and southern Catholics, no less
than any other group owned slaves. The majority of these
Catholic slaveholders were located in Maryland and Louisiana. They saw to it that their slaves were instructed in the
Faith and by 1863 it was estimated that there were approximately 100,000 Catholic slaves in the southern states.

Once war had been declared, Catholics joined both armies.
The Confederate troops were led by Catholic generals such as
P. G. T. Beauregard and William J. Hardee. They were opposed by Union troops led by Catholic generals such as Philip
H. Sheridan and William S. Rosecrans. Several dozen Catholic priests served as chaplains in both armies. The defeat of the
Confederacy left the southern states and their churches and
religious institutions in ruins. Although the governmental
union of the states was restored, many religious denominations—the Baptists and the Methodists, for example—remained divided after the war.

In 1866, the Catholic bishops of the United States gathered
at the Second Plenary Council of Baltimore to harmonize and
unify Catholic religious practice in the nation. (*See Reading
No. 16.*) The event received national attention and even President Andrew Johnson attended the closing ceremonies. During the two weeks of deliberations, the bishops clarified a
number of theological issues and reemphasized their collegial
role as leaders of the Church in the United States. In their
pastoral letter to the laity, the bishops emphasized the need for
more social institutions and exhorted their followers to evan-
gelize among the millions of newly freed slaves.

The two decades after the war marked a renewal of the
waves of Catholic immigration from Europe. The postwar preoccupation of American Catholic leaders was the same as it
had been before the Civil War—how to provide for the mil-

lions of new immigrants in need of assistance. The bishops exhorted their flocks to build more churches and called upon religious order to establish and staff Catholic social institutions for the aid of these new Catholics. The growth was as chaotic as it was endless.

The lack of order and structure within the American Church in the 1870s began to concern the Vatican. An 1878 report confirmed many of the worst fears of papal officials—the American Church was in need of improved organization and administration. Among the major problems identified in the report were favoritism in the appointment of bishops, too much emphasis on financial matters and not enough on pastoral care, and a general disregard or ignorance of canon law in the administration of dioceses. Rome began a campaign for a plenary council to rectify these matters.

Such a council was not convened until November, 1884. The delay was due, in part, to resistance by some bishops to the meddling of the Vatican in American Church affairs. Once it was held, however, the Third Plenary Council of Baltimore proved to be very productive. Among its achievements, the council codified canon law in the administration of American dioceses, proposed a national Catholic University, commissioned the compilation of national catechism, and mandated the establishment of parochial schools in each parish. (*See Reading No. 17.*) The most important accomplishment was that the legislation promulgated at the council would guide the American Church for the next thirty-five years.

CONCLUSION. From the perspective of 1885, the development of the Church in the United States during the previous thirty-five years must have seemed similar to its development during its first forty years. The years from 1789 to 1829 had been dominated by immigration, a lack of institutional resources, lay-clerical conflicts, and questions about American loyalty to American principles. These issues also dominated the years from 1830 to 1885.

Although the middle years of the nineteenth century were not a reprise of an earlier time, many of the issues were similar, but the scale of the problems was different. The growth of the Catholic community, for example, was extraordinary and every problem was magnified by this growth. Such an influx of new communicants—the majority of them Irish or German—overwhelmed almost every diocese. Bishops were forced to plead to their colleagues in Europe to send priests, nuns, and money to provide for this transplanted flock. With regular infusions from Europe, American bishops were able to provide for these immigrant Catholics, but at a high price.

Massive immigration and the subsequent recruitment of foreign-born religious to work in America diminished the ties of American Catholicism to its colonial past. Although it had been an American tradition since 1634, Catholicism appeared to be a foreign religion in America by the mid-nineteenth century. Catholic leaders faced the dilemma of insuring that their communicants would remain loyal to Catholicism, but at the same time become loyal, productive Americans. This issue also would be the central concern of the next generation of American Catholics.

CHAPTER 6

CATHOLICISM AND AMERICANISM, 1885–1908

The rapid expansion in the size of the American Catholic community that took place in the middle years of the nineteenth century was only a prelude to a second period of even greater growth. From 1885 to 1924, additional millions of Europeans, the majority of them Catholic, streamed into eastern seaports. Within a short time, every Catholic community in the United States was dominated by a new generation of foreign-born communicants.

Not surprisingly, these new immigrants added to existing tensions between the practice of Catholicism and the American way of life. The new Catholics, who came from Italy, Poland, and other eastern European countries, spoke little or no English and clung to the trappings of their native cultures. Though a vast majority of American Catholics professed a devout loyalty to the United States, and many Catholics had died in the Civil War, the denomination was tarred with the accusation of being un-American because of its large number of foreign-born communicants.

The arrival of millions of new Catholics was not the only issue facing American Catholicism during these years. Indeed, American Catholic leaders struggled to answer a series of serious and complex questions facing Catholicism in American society. How should the Church respond to the rapid industrialization in the American economy and its impact on the Catholic workingman? How quickly should these new Catholics be expected to abandon ethnic ways and become American? Should the Church take an active part in the political process? The answers to these questions eventually divided the American Catholic bishops into liberal and conservative factions. The bishops argued with one another on how to respond to the opportunities and temptations of the American way of life. It was a struggle that eventually reached a conclusion in the so-called ''Americanism'' controversy.

AMERICAN CATHOLIC SOCIETY. American Catholic society underwent another transformation in the years from 1885 to 1924. Once a denomination of Irish laborers and German farmers, American Catholicism became more of a cosmopolitan and multinational denomination, as Italians, Croatians, Bohemians, Slovaks, Lithuanians, and Poles flocked to the United States seeking a new life. From 1899 to 1924, the country accepted over 3.8 million Italians, nearly 1.5 million Poles, over 500,000 Slovaks and almost 500,000 Croatians, over 250,000 Lithuanians, and some 160,000 Bohemians. This mass migration radically changed the membership of the American Church, and in the process created substantial problems for a denomination already fractured by interethnic rivalries.

These foreigners struggled to sustain their Old World religion in their new country. Their Catholicism was a rural, conservative, intimate religion that had not changed for hundreds of years and this continuity with the past provided spiritual strength in a strange new land. It is no surprise, therefore, that these new Catholics worked to establish national parishes as the Germans had done in the previous generation. (*See Reading No. 21.*)

Although not pleased with this development, the bishops had little choice but to accept these new parishes as part of their motley dioceses. ''The sheer necessity of building churches at a rate rapid enough to bring the Mass within reach of the incoming tides of newcomers,'' notes historian Sam Bass Warner in his book *The Urban Wilderness,* ''delivered much of the power of the organization into the hands of the parish.''* The bishops needed the support of these new Catholics, and to get it, these prelates had to accept national parishes.

As an important part of their national parishes, the new Catholics sustained schools taught in their native languages. Unlike the local public schools, these ethnic parochial schools offered the promise of educating immigrant children without

---

*Sam Bass Warner, Jr., *The Urban Wilderness: A History of the American City* (New York, 1972) p. 163.

jeopardizing their spiritual salvation or their cultural heritage. For this reason many immigrant parents contributed their hard-earned dollars for the establishment and support of parish schools.

Not all of the new Catholics responded in quite the same way to the American Church. All the ethnic groups established national parishes, but not all the groups established parochial schools. The Poles, Slovaks, and Lithuanians, for example, were ardent supporters of the parochial school. However, the Italians and the Bohemians largely resisted the call for a separate school system, much to the consternation of local bishops. This independent spirit became known as the "Italian problem," a code phrase for rebellion and resistance to the American bishops.

Even though it was very popular with many new Catholics, the national parish with its ethnic parochial school was a transitional institution. Americanization was inevitable. It was assumed by the bishops that national parishes and ethnic schools would die out as these new Catholics acclimated themselves to American society. "Ours is the American Church," noted Archbishop John Ireland of St. Paul, Minnesota, "not Irish, German, Italian or Polish—and we will keep it American."

It was World War I, with its propaganda campaigns against all things foreign that ended the toleration of national parishes. The American public in general and the Catholic hierarchy in particular would no longer accept the claim of the new Catholics that they could maintain their native languages and customs and still be loyal to their new nation. The American public rejected the argument as contradictory and pressured the foreign-born to pledge openly their total allegiance to the United States. National parishes and foreign language schools were casualties of this loyalty campaign.

CATHOLIC-PROTESTANT CONFLICT. Reaction to the arrival of millions of immigrant Catholics was mixed among the American public. Many Americans were dismayed at the poverty, illiteracy, and criminality among these new arrivals—that they were Catholic was yet another concern. The Church hierarchy was becoming increasingly vocal on public issues and a surprising number of Catholics in major cities were winning elective office as mayors and congress-men. Many patriotic Americans wanted to know what could be done to limit the influence of these new immigrants and their foreign religion on the American way of life.

For some of these zealous citizens the answer was to attack Catholicism. Dozens of secret, patriotic, fraternal organiza-tions emerged in the 1880s with the expressed purpose of "exposing" foreigners and their religion as anti-American. These groups, led by the virulently anti-Catholic American Protective Association, accused the Church of fomenting un-rest between workers and management, of undermining the public schools, and of conspiring to destroy American liber-ties. It has been estimated that the American Protective Asso-ciation had a cumulative enrollment of half a million members in the 1890s. The popularity and influence of the APA was as short-lived as it was meteoric. The organization was largely discredited after 1910 for its outlandish claims of papal plots and was divided by internal bickering.

The beginning of the progressive movement in American politics gave the public greater confidence that immigrants could actually be absorbed into the general populace. Catho-lics and non-Catholics could even share an occasional laugh over the foibles of immigrant Catholic life. "Martin J. Dooley," a fictional Irish Catholic saloon-keeper created by Finley Peter Dunne, was one of the nation's most popular newspaper characters at the turn of the century. (*See Reading No. 20.*) The progressives were confident that social settle-ments and public schools would assist these largely urban im-migrants to adjust and adapt to the American way of life.

This is not to say that all foreign and anti-Catholic agitation had died out. The Junior-United American Mechanics, an anti-Catholic and antiforeign organization founded in the 1890s, saw its membership jump from 147,000 in 1901 to 224,000 only a decade later. Generally, however, during the years from 1900 to 1910, anti-Catholic agitation languished.

NATIONAL CHURCH LEADERSHIP. The years from 1886 to 1908 were an era of energetic individualism within the American Catholic leadership. The bishops differed with one another over a variety of social issues that defined the relationship between Catholicism and American society. Should the Church condemn labor unions? Could the clergy speak out on political matters? Should the Church take direct steps to Americanize its growing flock? What position should the Church take on public education? The contest was not for the leadership of diocesan or parish affairs, it was for the right to define better the Catholic Church's place in American society.

Although the Catholic bishops would have disdained labels, there was a division within the Catholic hierarchy along traditional liberal-conservative lines during these years. The liberals, led by Archbishop John Ireland of St. Paul and Cardinal James Gibbons of Baltimore looked for ways of strengthening the ties between Catholicism and American social values. On the other end of the spectrum were the conservatives led by Archbishop Michael Corrigan of New York and Bishop Bernard McQuaid of Rochester, who argued that group solidarity and the preservation of religious faith must be maintained at any cost even if the price divided Catholics from the rest of American society. In truth, the conservatives were deeply suspicious of democratic ideas, believing that such ideas would undermine the Catholic faith.

The first issue faced by the bishops was the matter of labor unions. Many of the men involved in organizing unions in the 1880s were Catholics, just as the workers themselves were Catholics. Would the American bishops support or condemn these efforts? The Knights of Labor, the largest and most prominent American labor union had been condemned by the Catholic hierarchy in Canada, but it was unclear what position would be taken by the American bishops. Assured that the Knights were not a secret society and that the unions opposed boycotts and closed shops, six of the nine archbishops voted against condemnation in a meeting in Baltimore in 1886, but the vote was not unanimous which meant that a final decision had to be left to the Vatican.

To ensure that the Pope would sustain the majority view, Cardinal Gibbons took up the matter with Vatican officials while in Rome in 1887. In a carefully worded statement that had been prepared in large part by his liberal colleagues, Gibbons argued that "to lose the heart of the people would be a misfortune for which the friendship of the few rich and powerful would be no compensation." (*See Reading No. 18.*) The Pope agreed and the American hierarchy gained the reputation for supporting the working man.

A second point of confrontation between the liberals and the conservatives was the canonical status of ethnic groups in the United States. For years the Germans had complained that the loss of native languages meant the loss of religious faith. The issue became more intense as German Catholic priests in this country began to agitate for more canonical authority for national parishes. Yet a crisis did not emerge until a well-intentioned German Catholic layman named Peter Paul Cahensley petitioned the Pope for the appointment of foreign bishops to minister specifically to his countrymen in the United States.

Cahensley headed an international mission organization based in Germany, known as the St. Raphael Society. At a meeting in Switzerland in 1890, representatives of several European branches of the society met and prepared a formal petition that asked the Pope to intercede on the part of immigrant Catholics in the United States. The petition was eventually signed by fifty-one representatives from seven nations; it was presented personally by Cahensley to Pope Leo XIII in April 1891.

This international interference in American Catholic affairs deeply concerned the majority of American bishops. Only the handful of German-American bishops saw any merit in the proposal. Other conservative bishops—usually the allies of the German-Americans—fell silent. The fact that the Pope quickly dismissed the plan as impractical and unnecessary did not matter. Liberals such as Ireland and Gibbons continued to use "Cahensleyism" as a rallying cry in their effort to Americanize the foreign elements within the Church.

The third disagreement within the Catholic hierarchy was more serious and substantive than labor unions and national parishes. Indeed, the conflict between liberal and conservative bishops over public and parochial education was a bitter one. All these men—regardless of their philosophical viewpoint—agreed that Catholic schooling was a necessity if the Church was to survive and flourish in Protestant America. Beyond that simple commitment, however, these men could agree on little else. Were parish schools an unfortunate necessity or a shining moral alternative to godless public schools? As long as this question was not raised in public there was peace between the liberals and the conservatives.

The peace was broken by Archbishop John Ireland when he proposed a plan for the schools in certain select communities to be administered jointly by church and state. Even more shocking was that he proposed the plan publicly at a meeting of the National Education Association in 1890 and put the plan into action by signing agreements with the public school boards of Fairbault and Stillwater, Minnesota. Henceforth the parish schools of those communities would be operated by the public school boards during the traditional school day. The teachers—all Catholics—would be paid by the boards to teach the standard secular subjects. After hours, however, the schools would revert to the parishes for use in religious instruction and other activities.

The uproar caused by the plan was heard across the country and all the way to Rome. (*See Reading No. 19.*) Acrimonious "debate" raged in the Catholic press; pamphlets were published defending and attacking both the general concept and the specific plan. The controversy raged throughout 1891 and 1892 with no sign of abating. To end it all, the Pope released a diplomatic statement praising the conservatives for their fine work in establishing parochial schools, but also noting that the "Fairbault Plan" could be "tolerated." Surprisingly even a papal letter could not end the matter; conservatives led by Corrigan and McQuaid continued to press their attack on the plan. It took a special papal emissary and a second papal letter to settle the controversy. Corrigan and the conservatives finally accepted the Pope's decision to allow cooperative school plans, but with bitterness and resignation.

Yet the school controversy was not the most serious conflict between the liberals and the conservatives. That incident was the dispute over the publication of a French translation of a biography of Isaac Hecker, the American Catholic social philosopher and founder of the Congregation of St. Paul. The book included an introduction by Archbishop Ireland that praised Hecker for his contributions to the Church in America.

The book itself had a curious publishing history. It had been published in both serial and book form in the United States in 1891 without a hint of trouble. There was nothing in the biography that was out of the ordinary. To be sure, the book emphasized Hecker's efforts to harmonize Catholic principles with American democratic traditions, but Ireland, Gibbons, and other liberals had been making the same points for more than a decade and these ideas had been largely accepted by the Vatican.

Certainly the liberals in the United States were not prepared to have these ideas labeled as "heresy" when the Hecker biography was translated and published in French in 1897. The book was the spark of a controversy that raged in Europe and the United States. Liberals in France had used the book to call for an effort to modernize the Church in France. French conservatives attacked the book, claiming that Hecker was the victim of delusions and that his ideas and those of his liberal colleagues in America were nothing short of heresy. This time the conservatives got the ear of the Vatican. Something had to be done about the ideology known throughout Europe as "Americanism."

Pope Leo XIII appointed a commission to sort out the truth and the result was a papal letter addressed to Cardinal Gibbons that condemned certain ideas, but praised the American Church. The letter made clear that there was no common definition for "Americanism." Dated January 22, 1899, *Testem Benevolentiae,* as the letter was called, summarized the European notion of Americanism—that the Church should abandon ancient traditions and become more modern in its theological and social viewpoints. If this is what was meant by "Americanism" then it was to be condemned as heresy, but Leo was careful not to impugn Hecker or accuse the American liberals of heresy. It was a cautious letter that acknowledged the claims of both sides.

Testem Benevolentiae effectively ended the Americanist controversy and it also took the momentum out of the efforts of Archbishop Ireland, Cardinal Gibbons and the other liberals to establish bridges between Catholicism and American democracy. Both the liberals and the conservatives claimed vindication in the letter, but in effect it accomplished more for the conservatives. After 1900, the liberals' efforts to modernize the Church came to an end.

Indeed, the very concept of "modernism" was condemned by a new Pope, Pius X, in the 1907 encyclical *Pascendi Dominici Gregis*. This papal letter condemned the implicit error of any effort to reconcile Catholicism with the scientific and scholarly inquiries of the twentieth century. The Pope called for his bishops to be vigilant in looking for "modernism" in their respective dioceses. By 1910, the Pope had gone so far as to impose an oath against modernism on all priests and seminarians. In short, intellectual renewal was condemned as nothing short of heresy.

This encyclical had a chilling effect on liberal Catholicism in America. Reading between the lines of the encyclical, it was clear that the new Pope considered "Americanism" to be one aspect of the modernist crisis. Intellectual inquiry came to an abrupt halt at American Catholic seminaries and universities; faculty members were dismissed and scholarly journals shut down. "Free intellectual inquiry in ecclesiastical circles came to a virtual stand still," notes historian Michael Gannon, "It was as though someone had pulled a switch and the lights had failed all across the American landscape."*

The early years of the twentieth century also marked another shift in the status of the American Church. In June 1908, the Pope issued a notification that the Church in the United States was no longer a mission territory under the jurisdiction of the Vatican. Henceforth, the American Church would have the same canonical status as the Church in Italy, France, or Germany. American bishops could make decisions for their dioceses without the direct oversight of the Vatican.

There was a clear irony in the Pope's recognition of the maturity of American Catholicism. On the one hand his attacks against modernism showed a lack of faith in his American flock; on the other hand, he recognized that American Catholicism was among the most robust branches of the Church and should be allowed to govern its own affairs. This ambiguity would become the hallmark of the relationship be-

---

*Michael V. Gannon, "Before and After Modernism: The Intellectual Isolation of the American Priest," in John Tracy Ellis, ed., *The Catholic Priest in the United States* (Collegeville, MN, 1971) p. 341.

tween the Vatican and the American Church for the next several decades.

CONCLUSION. The twenty-five years spanning the beginning of the twentieth century were years of conflict for American Catholicism. The hierarchy struggled to define the proper balance between Catholicism and American values. Liberals such as Cardinal James Gibbons and Archbishop John Ireland sought new ways to strengthen the ties between Catholicism and Americanism, while conservatives, led by Archbishop Michael Corrigan, were suspicious of American culture and feared that the process of becoming American would undermine the religious faith of many Catholics.

There also was conflict between Catholics and other Americans. Most Americans were deeply concerned about the distinctive foreign overtones of Catholicism in America. Patriotic pronouncements of loyalty from various Catholic groups did not ease the tension. Many Catholics in America still seemed to cling to their native cultures; as long as they did so, they were not "American" in the eyes of most non-Catholics. At its most extreme, these concerns were reflected in the growth and development of a number of anti-Catholic organizations and publications.

Yet these years also marked the emergence of a mature American Church. Its growth in numbers and its wealth were sufficient for the Vatican to remove it from missionary status and place the American Church on an equal status with the Church in other nations. Catholicism in America had come of age.

CHAPTER 7

THE SEARCH FOR ORDER AND IDENTITY, 1908–1945

The first half of the twentieth century was something of an odyssey for American Catholicism. Most American Catholics were shedding their immigrant identities, but they had not yet been accepted as being fully American by non-Catholics. Individually and collectively, Catholics worked during these years to define more clearly their role and their place in twentieth-century American society.

At the core of this new definition was organization as the Church in the United States embraced wholeheartedly the American concepts of business administration. On a national level, the bishops expanded their National Catholic Welfare Conference to become their administrative arm and to provide a national voice for their collective concerns. On a local level, a new generation of bishops used modern administrative and business practices to restructure and reorganize their diocesan operations. The concepts of efficiency and economy were added to the ethos of American Catholicism.

In addition to revamping the administrative structure of the American Church, Catholics also sought to discover their place in public life. The bigotry of the Ku Klux Klan became increasingly popular in the 1920s, and even more, typical Americans questioned whether Catholics could ever be loyal Americans. In response to various acts of anti-Catholicism, Catholics petitioned the U.S. Supreme Court for the protection of their rights as American citizens. In *Pierce v. Society of Sisters* (1925), for example, the Supreme Court upheld the right of Catholic parents to send their children to parochial schools. Catholic loyalties also were called into question in 1928 when Governor Alfred E. Smith of New York, a Catholic, was selected as the Democratic Party's nominee for President. Many Americans continued to believe that it was not possible for a Catholic to be faithful to both his religion and his nation.

American Catholicism also was defined by the three major

historical events during these years. Certainly the response of Catholics to World War I in the 1910s, the Great Depression of the 1930s, and World War II in the 1940s helped to clarify the possibilities and limits of Catholic participation in public life. Catholics were among the most ardent supporters of the effort to win the "Great War" in Europe in 1918. They also were active in President Franklin D. Roosevelt's New Deal programs in the 1930s as more Catholics served in government during these years than at any time previously. When the call to war came a second time this century, young Catholics joined the armed forces with the encouragement and blessings of their parents, pastors, and bishops.

AMERICAN CATHOLIC SOCIETY. The years from 1908 to 1945 were characterized by alternating waves of crisis and confidence. The 1910s were shaped by war in Europe which forced many foreign-born and ethnic Catholics to abandon their native cultures and embrace their adopted homelands. Wartime loyalty campaigns, in concert with the efforts of local bishops, were the death knell of national parishes and foreign language schools. Young Catholics were encouraged to think of themselves as American and join the war effort against the evil "Huns" of Germany.

Yet this wartime experience did not transform ethnic Catholics into full-fledged Americans. They were no longer foreigners, to be sure, but neither were they completely American. Catholics living in America in the first half of the twentieth century were "marginal" citizens unsure of their identity. They would work during the years from 1920 to 1950 to establish their place and that of their religion in American society. It would be no small task.

This is not to say that American Catholics were alienated or disaffected during these years. In fact, the 1920s were years of optimism for American Catholics. The decade was one of prosperity and employment and Catholics enjoyed their share of both. The majority of Catholics were the sons and daughters of immigrants who had achieved a level of personal wealth that was beyond their expectations; they now had the resources to help their children obtain better schooling and employment than the previous generation of Catholics. A significant number of young Catholics attended colleges and moved into management positions in American corporations. Even though the Ku Klux Klan and other hate groups caused some general apprehension within the Catholic community, anti-Catholicism was not a part of the lives of most American Catholics.

What Catholics of the 1920s did not immediately perceive was the changing contours of the Catholic population. For more than a century, the growth of Catholicism had been fueled by numerous influxes of immigrants from Europe. This growth came to an end in 1924 when a new immigration law put strict quotas on the numbers of immigrants allowed into the United States. With the floodgates closed, the rate of growth of the American Catholic population abated somewhat and Catholicism shed its ethnic identity.

Several factors worked to breakdown the national parish, the bastion of Catholic ethnicity. Catholics who were born in America spurned the romantic nationalism and foreign culture of their parents. Ethnic ghettos broke down as these Catholics moved to new homes in the suburbs where cultural origins did not determine residence. Old neighborhoods changed hands as one ethnic group left and another moved in and it was not unusual for a parish to pass from the Irish to the Italians to the blacks in the course of a century. Finally, ethnicity also was undermined by a concerted campaign for Americanization undertaken by the Catholic hierarchy during and after World War I. By the end of World War II, Catholics thought of themselves as Americans of Irish or Italian descent rather than as Irish-Americans or Italian-Americans.

NATIONAL CHURCH LEADERSHIP. Rapid growth and change within all areas of American life generally and within the Church in particular precipitated a desire to bring more order to Catholic affairs on both the diocesan and national levels. Bishops began to use modern methods of accounting and business administration to manage their dioceses. They employed articulate young priests to monitor, centralize, and tighten control over diocesan affairs. Various Catholic interest groups also established national associations to bring order to their efforts to influence public opinion. Professional associations for Catholic educators, physicians, lawyers, and historians were among those established during these years.

Catholics also began to look beyond their own borders during the first decades of the twentieth century. Young American Catholics entering the religious life served as missionaries in Latin America, Africa, and the Orient. This commitment was symbolized in the 1911 establishment of the first American religious order devoted to the foreign missions. *(See Reading No. 22.)*

No event affected national Church leadership as much as World War I. The 1917 decision of the American government to join the Allies in Europe was followed by an appeal to patriotism. Religious denominations across the land were urged to support the boys "over there." With more than a million young Catholics in uniform, Catholic leaders were determined to support their nation, but how? The answer was a national organization under the aegis of the nation's bishops. With the approval of Cardinal Gibbons, 115 delegates from sixty-eight dioceses and twenty-seven societies met in August 1917 to organize the "National Catholic War Council." Father John J. Burke, editor of *The Catholic World* and founder of the Chaplains' Aid Association, was picked to head the new organization. Four bishops were chosen to serve as an oversight committee for the NCWC.

The NCWC had a short-term goal of coordinating Catholic war activities, but it quickly became clear to Burke, Gibbons, and other bishops that such a national organization would be a positive boon to the American Catholic hierarchy after the war. Burke and his colleagues worked hard to convince the Vatican that such a national organization would not be a threat to the authority of the Pope. After some vacillation, the Vatican finally approved the NCWC, but not before emphasizing the noncouncilor character of the organization by changing a "council" into a "conference." The National Catholic Welfare Conference, continues to function to this day as the United States Catholic Conference by giving administrative support to the American Catholic bishops.

Perhaps the most substantive and lasting contribution of the war council was a social action statement known as the

"Bishops' Program of Social Reconstruction." This landmark statement was written by Father John A. Ryan, the foremost Catholic social philosopher of the first half of the twentieth century. It laid out a blueprint for social reform that would later be implemented during the "New Deal" of President Franklin D. Roosevelt. The program urged more federal involvement in the workplace, favored the establishment of minimum wages for all workers, opposed child labor, and proposed equal pay for women doing equal work with men. The plan also urged more collaboration between labor and management. The bishops gave their approval to this pathbreaking document—the first major policy statement by the Catholic bishops since the Third Plenary Council in 1884. (*See Reading No.23.*)

The 1920s and 1930s were decades of consolidation and unification for the leaders of the Church. After several decades of internecine warfare over the proper course for the Church, and a search for order that led to the establishment of the National Catholic Welfare Conference, the American Catholic bishops completed modernization of the bureaucracy for which twentieth-century American Catholicism became famous in the 1950s.

This campaign to modernize administrative controls over Church affairs was part of the collective management style of a new generation of prelates who were determined to run their dioceses with economy and efficiency. A collective portrait of the men who headed the twelve largest dioceses in the United States in 1920 reveals many shared characteristics. Unlike the generation that had preceded them, these new bishops (eleven of twelve) were American-born, and a majority had been trained in Rome. Of Irish heritage for the most part, they served long tenures, averaging over twenty-five years of service.

Historian Edward R. Kantowicz, in his biography of Cardinal George Mundelein of Chicago, has evaluated the leadership styles of these men and found five common elements—giantism, going first class, business-like administration, "Americanism," and political influence. Giantism was a reflection of Catholic insecurity; whenever the bishops established new institutions or got involved in construction, they built on a massive scale. New seminaries and cathedrals were common in these dioceses. These bishops also were determined to go first class in everything that they did—they loved pageantry and ceremony, good food, and stimulating conversation. Yet these men were not dilettantes and they ran their dioceses with the most modern management practices culled from American business. Both individually and collectively, they never missed an opportunity to profess their undying love of America and American values. Finally, they cultivated contacts with national political leaders—presidents, congressmen, governors—as a means of protecting the interests of the Church. "Builders, administrators, politicos, anti-intellectuals, and chauvinist patriots," notes Kantowicz, "their leadership was crude but effective. They put the Church on the map."*

The nature of Church leadership during these years also was affected by the growing influence of the National Catholic Welfare Conference. Although the role of the conference was strictly advisory, staff members spoke with authority; the conference gave the American bishops a national voice. Throughout the 1920s when the Church was attacked by anti-Catholic bigots, and during the depression of the 1930s, the conference played a powerful and influential role in influencing the public opinion of Catholicism.

CATHOLIC–PROTESTANT CONFLICT. The troubled relationship between Catholics and Protestants continued into the twentieth century. The early years of the century were a period of relative calm; overt anti-Catholicism seemed to have disappeared after the demise of the American Protective Association, but a renewed campaign against Catholics emerged in the 1910s, this time in the South, a region with few Catholics. The attack was spearheaded by Tom Watson of Georgia, who used his popular *Watson's Magazine* to attack the Pope, Catholic priests, and the Knights of Columbus. Watson was joined by a Missourian named Wilbur Phelps,

---

*Edward R. Kantowicz, *Corporation Sole: Cardinal Mundelein and Chicago Catholicism* (Notre Dame, 1983) p. 5.

who used his patriotic weekly, *The Menace,* for the same purpose. From 1912 to 1914, a number of other anti-Catholic publications appeared in Minnesota, North Carolina, Indiana, and Arkansas, but none was as popular as *The Menace.* This brand of anti-Catholicism was distinctly rural and largely southern. Few readers of *Watson's Magazine* or *The Menace* had ever met a Catholic.

Some Americans feared that the foreign ties of many Catholics made them disloyal Americans and various hate groups played upon these fears. The circulation of *The Menace* reached a high point of 1.5 million readers in 1915. Several state legislatures became so concerned about Catholicism that they considered measures to inspect and supervise Catholic social institutions such as schools and hospitals. In New York, an "American Party" candidate for governor, running on an anti-Catholic platform, showed surprising strength in upstate counties. This sudden recurrence of anti-Catholicism deeply concerned the American bishops; it appeared that the country was returning to the hate-filled years of the 1890s.

Anti-Catholicism began to decline after 1915, and the circulation of *The Menace* dropped dramatically as the public shifted its attention to building unity for the war effort. Personal differences had to be set aside so that the nation could defeat "the forces of evil" in Europe. The Catholic hierarchy responded positively to these campaigns by stressing that Catholicism was a thoroughly American religion. More than a million young Catholic men proved their loyalty by fighting for America on the fields of France.

Catholic service in World War I did not obliterate anti-Catholicism in America. In fact, prejudice against Catholics reemerged in the 1920s in new and vicious forms. The Ku Klux Klan, a racist organization with roots in the Civil War era, recruited more than two million members in the 1920s, most of them in large cities with substantial Catholic populations. The Klan attacked any and all things Catholic, accusing the Church of being fundamentally un-American. As ridiculous as the Klan's charges were, millions of Americans listened and believed; throughout the 1920s, Catholicism was again under attack.

At the root of the Catholic-Protestant conflict during these

years was the relationship between church and state under the
Constitution. Could the state require all children to attend public schools? Could a Catholic be loyal to both his church and
his country if elected to serve as President? Should the United
States send an ambassador to Vatican City, recognized by
many nations as a secular state? These were among the questions that were raised during the 1920s and 1930s.

The first questions to be addressed concerned education. In
1920, Catholics were active in opposing legislation to provide
direct federal aid to public education. Catholics argued publicly that such aid would be an undue interference in state and
local affairs, but privately these same Catholics admitted that
their opposition stemmed, in part, from the fact that federal
aid was not offered to parochial schools as well as public
schools. The proposed legislation was defeated in 1920 and
subsequent years.

A more serious matter was the growing antagonism of the
state legislatures toward parochial education. Legislation under consideration in several states during the early 1920s
threatened the existence of parish schools. In 1922, when the
citizens of Oregon approved a referendum that would abolish
all parochial and private education, Catholics fought the law
all the way to the Supreme Court.

The law in question required parents to send their children
to public school until graduation from grade school. Parents
who did not comply, with few exceptions, would be subject to
fines, imprisonment, or both. Two Oregon private schools—
one Catholic and one secular—sued the state, arguing that the
law was unconstitutional. The plaintiffs were upheld in district
court and in subsequent appeals up to the Supreme Court.
"The fundamental theory of liberty upon which upon all governments of this union repose," noted the high Court, "excludes any general power of the state to standardize its children
by forcing them to accept instruction from public school
teachers only." This landmark decision, *Pierce v. Society of
Sisters,* was considered by many to be a bill of rights for
private education. *(See Reading No. 24.)*

A final aspect to the education question was state aid to
private schools. Only five years after it had upheld the right of
Catholic schools to exist, the Court upheld a Louisiana law

that provided school books to all children in the state attending either private or public schools. The Court agreed that such a law was in the best interest of the state and did not breach the wall separating church and state. "Individual interests are aided," noted the court, "only as the common interest is safeguarded." It was this decision *(Cochran v. Louisiana)* which encouraged Catholics to think that other forms of state aid also might be ruled constitutional.

State aid for parochial schools was one question, but could a practicing Catholic serve as President of the United States? How could any man serve two masters—the Church and the Constitution? The question first became a serious issue at the 1924 Democratic National Convention, when the name of Alfred E. Smith of New York was placed in nomination for the presidency. Smith, a practicing Catholic, had been a very successful governor and a logical choice for the nomination except for his religion. The conservative elements of the party deadlocked the convention and in Smith's place they finally nominated compromise candidate John W. Davis on the 103rd ballot.

Smith would not bow to prejudice. He refused to believe that he would be rejected by the voters simply because he was a Catholic and he faced the religion issue head-on in an exchange of articles with attorney Charles G. Marshall in the pages of *The Atlantic Monthly*. Marshall charged that it was virtually impossible for a Catholic to reconcile the Church's religious tenets with the Constitution and the American principle of religious liberty. Smith replied without equivocation that Marshall was wrong, at least so far as Smith was concerned. "I recognize no power in the institutions of the Church," he noted, "to interfere with the operations of the Constitution of the United States or the enforcement of the law of the land." Smith thought naively that this would end the controversy over his religion. *(See Reading No. 25.)*

Smith was wrong, of course. He gained the Democratic nomination in 1928, but anti-Catholic zealots and even mainstream Protestants worked hard to deny him the highest office in the land. In a vicious, bitter campaign, Smith was attacked as a tool of the Vatican. He accepted his eventual defeat with honor. Deeply saddened by the bigotry and prejudice that had marked the campaign, Smith left public life to pursue wealth and fortune.

Smith's loss was a great disappointment to many of the nation's Catholics. They were as disheartened as Smith at the strength and persistence of anti-Catholicism in the country. They wondered how much longer it would be before the nation would set aside religion as a reason for excluding a man from the presidency. More important, how long would it be before the nation accepted Catholics as full-fledged citizens.

A final church-state question during these years had to do with the Vatican. The outbreak of war in Europe in 1939 precipitated a need for intelligence information on the part of the U.S. government. Not surprisingly, one of the best listening posts for such information was the Vatican, a neutral oasis in the middle of Fascist Italy. On Christmas Eve 1939, President Franklin D. Roosevelt wrote to Pope Pius XII: "It would give me great satisfaction to send to you my personal representative in order that our parallel endeavors for peace and the attenuation of suffering may be arrested." Roosevelt knew that it would be a controversial appointment.

As expected, a number of individuals and organizations protested that this special recognition of the Vatican was unconstitutional. To minimize the protest and the rancor, Roosevelt appointed Myron Taylor, a Protestant, to serve as his representative. The President gave him the rank of ambassador but did not submit his name to the Senate for confirmation. Taylor received no salary and his expenses were paid out of a special White House fund. As American involvement in the war became deeper and Taylor's presence at the Vatican more valuable, the protests died down. Taylor served as the President's representative to the Pope for the next decade.

The American involvement in World War II, temporarily ended the acrimony and argument between Catholics and Protestants. All Americans set aside their differences until democracy had once again been secured. This was one point on which all Catholics and Protestants could agree.

ECONOMIC DEPRESSION AND WORLD WAR. The worldwide economic depression that began in 1929 and continued for the next decade played no denominational favorites.

Catholic, Protestant and Jew alike suffered general hardship. Millions of Americans were unemployed and it was not clear what could or should be done to overcome the blight. One part of the solution came in 1933 after the election in 1932 of Franklin D. Roosevelt as President. His administration was heavily supported by American Catholics, who joined the Roosevelt administration in unprecedented numbers. Well-known Catholics such as James A. Farley, Thomas Walsh, and Frank Murphy were named to the Roosevelt cabinet, and thousands of other Catholics served in less visible government positions. One historian has estimated that a full quarter of Roosevelt's judicial appointments went to Catholics. Also among those Catholics assisting the President were two priests, John A. Ryan and Francis J. Haas, who sat on dozens of presidential boards and commissions.

Catholics also were active in reform efforts outside the Roosevelt administration. For example, Catholics took an active part in efforts to reform the American labor movement. The leadership of the newly-formed Congress of Industrial Organizations (CIO) included Catholics such as Philip Murray, James Carey, and John Brophy. The CIO leadership worked closely with the NCWC Social Action Department to implement *The Bishop's Program for Social Reconstruction* and the CIO membership included millions of Catholic workingmen and a large number of prolabor priests and bishops. Together, church and labor joined forces with the Roosevelt administration to work for a new economic order.

The unions were not the only organizations of workers to respond to the Great Depression. Calls for social action filled the pages of the Catholic press in the 1930s and dozens of groups were established to develop a *spiritual* response to the poverty and hardship of the times. These groups committed themselves to lives of prayer, sacrifice, and work among the poorest elements of American society.

One of the most important and lasting of the social action efforts was the Catholic Worker Movement. Begun in May 1933 by American journalist Dorothy Day and French social philosopher Peter Maurin, the Catholic Worker was a bit of everything—a social philosophy, a newspaper, a consortium of hospitality houses and farms, and above all a catalyst for change within the Church. (*See Reading No. 27.*)

Maurin was the philosopher of the movement, but Day was the driving force that made the Catholic Worker effective. It was Day who kept the newspaper going, and it was Day who saw to the support of the urban hospitality centers and the farming communes. Most of all, it was Dorothy Day's charisma or "presence" as one worker called it, that shaped a generation of Catholic activists who later would work for social change in the 1950s and 1960s. It is a testament to Day's influence that the Catholic Worker Movement continues to the present, carrying on the work of its founders.

Not all of the Catholic social philosophers of the 1930s could be considered liberals. The most powerful Catholic advocate of social change was a priest named Charles E. Coughlin, who became widely known for spellbinding speeches. Coughlin's rise to fame and influence began with a local radio program in Detroit in the late 1920s, and his ability to capture the spiritual and material concerns attracted a large national audience. His popularity was extraordinary; at one time in the 1930s, Coughlin employed over 100 secretaries to respond to his mail.

Coughlin did not start his radio career as a reactionary. During the early 1930s, he ardently supported the New Deal. "It's Roosevelt or ruin," he proclaimed, but the Roosevelt administration did not move quickly enough for Coughlin; he became increasingly critical of it and eventually joined other critics in establishing a third party. (*See Reading No. 26.*) Most disturbing about Coughlin, however, was the hatred and venom that gradually became a central part of his radio sermons; demagoguery and anti-Semitism became his stock in trade. By the time he was finally silenced in the early 1940s, Coughlin was little more than a fascist hate-monger, an embarrassment to his Church.

Coughlin was something of a phenomenon. Although he had a large and devoted following, his views on the Roosevelt administration and the New Deal were not representative of the Catholic population in general. The same Catholics who listened to Coughlin each week, continued to vote for Roosevelt term after term.

The one area where Catholics parted with FDR was foreign policy. As Europe was engulfed in war in 1939, Roosevelt moved to assist the Allies and many Catholics disagreed with his policy. Some, such as Dorothy Day, were pacifists, but other Catholics were isolationists who believed that this was Europe's war and America should stay out of it. Roosevelt was not without some Catholic support, of course, but it was weak at best. Catholic loyalty to the Roosevelt administration generally was restricted to domestic programs.

Once war was declared, however, Catholics eagerly joined the armed forces and served with distinction. Regardless of their views on specific foreign policies, American Catholics were patriots and the defense of the nation was the duty of every patriot. Historian James Hennesey estimates that Catholics constituted between twenty-five and thirty-five percent of the armed forces during the war, a percentage significantly higher than their percentage of the population. The bishops supported this participation individually and collectively in their annual pastoral letter of 1942. *(See Reading No. 28.)* As was the case with all of America's wars, Catholics sought to prove their loyalty through bravery on the battlefield. World War II was no exception.

CONCLUSION. The first half of the twentieth century was a time of transformation for American Catholicism. The Church was shedding the last vestiges of its foreign overtones and searching for a distinctive American identity. American Catholics seemed to have the same goals and beliefs as other Americans, yet they were not quite the same. There was that lingering question: how could a Catholic be truly loyal to both the Pope and the Constitution? In spite of their wartime service and other contributions, many Americans still did not think it was possible for practicing Catholics to be fully American.

This generation of Catholics refused to be rebuffed by such a view of their religion. Throughout the first half of the century, Catholics took an increasingly active role in American society. Beginning with *The Bishop's Program for Social Reconstruction,* through Al Smith's campaign for the presidency, to Catholic participation in the Roosevelt administration, Catholics were more actively involved in American society in the 1920s and 1930s than at any previous time. Even if some Americans could not accept them as good citizens, Catholics were determined to make their mark on American society.

CHAPTER 8

ACHIEVING THE AMERICAN DREAM,
1945–1960

The end of World War II brought with it a new resolve among American Catholics to integrate themselves fully into American society. Young Catholic veterans returned from war to attend college, win well-paying jobs with American corporations, buy homes in the suburbs, build new parishes, and participate in community affairs. A significant number of Catholics became affluent and it was not unusual to hear of Catholic millionaires in almost every diocese. By almost any standard, Catholics were one of the most successful segments within American society.

Yet Catholics still found themselves to be outsiders on church-state issues and these differences were serious enough to precipitate significant interdenominational tension during the late 1940s and early 1950s. Catholics argued with other Americans over public aid to parochial schools, the appointment of an ambassador to the Vatican, and related church-state matters. On several occasions during these years the Supreme Court attempted to clarify the relationship between church and state, but to little avail. As late as the mid-1950s, Catholics and Protestants could not find much common ground.

A large measure of the tension dissipated in the latter half of the 1950s as continued socio-economic mobility and educational achievement brought American Catholics in more frequent contact with Americans of other faiths. Catholics and Protestants came to know and understand one another better and suspicion gave way to toleration. The election of an open and friendly Pope, John XXIII, gave the Church a new, less forbidding image and eased Protestant concerns. Certainly the most dramatic evidence that Catholics and Protestants had overcome their differences was the election of John F. Kennedy in 1960, the first Catholic President.

AMERICAN CATHOLIC SOCIETY. The fifteen years from 1945 to 1960 witnessed a quiet revolution in the status of the American Catholic population. Catholics became more visible during these years because there were more of them. The U.S. census of 1940 had identified 21.4 million Catholics, an impressive increase of 3.6 million over the 1920 total. Yet no census taker or demographer could have predicted that the size of the Catholic community would double by 1960 when the census revealed 42 million Catholics! This increase is even more impressive since the years of massive immigration had ended in 1924.

Size was not the only aspect of change within the Catholic community. As early as 1940, sociologists began to study a shift in Catholic self-identification as a new generation shed their ethnic identities; it was a shift that allowed for interethnic marriage but did not undermine religious identity. Thus, it was not unusual for Catholic babies born in the postwar years to have a mixed ethnic heritage, Irish and Italian, Polish and German. The shift in the Catholic community away from interethnic rivalries was additional evidence that ghetto walls were coming down.

These young Catholics were on the move. They wanted a good life for themselves and their children and like tens of millions of other Americans of all denominations, they flocked to the new suburban communities on the edges of major American cities. The ethnic and religious organizations and social institutions that marked Catholics as foreigners were on the decline. Young Catholics now lived in neighborhoods of mixed nationalities and mixed religions.

However, the move to the suburbs did not precipitate a loss of faith. The 1950s witnessed a nationwide "revival of religion" among all religious denominations and Catholics were no exception. New Catholic parishes, named after long-forgotten saints, emerged simultaneous with new subdivisions. Not surprisingly, the central concern of most of these suburban parishes was finances. Week after week suburban pastors exhorted their flocks to give more to the church building fund or the fund drive for the new school. Historian Jay P. Dolan notes that it was not unusual for half of the

Sunday sermons in a typical suburban parish to be devoted to finances.*

There was also a sharp increase in religious devotion, public piety, and vocations. Catholics of all ages attended Mass and other religious exercises in extraordinary numbers. Young couples participated in the Cana Conference and the Christian Family Movement to strengthen the spiritual life within the home. Catholics, generally, were moved by stories of religious conversion and missionary work that appeared in the Catholic newspapers, books, and magazines that many Catholics received in their homes each week.

This trend toward spirituality was nurtured by a handful of priests experienced in the use of television and radio. Dynamic priests such as Father James Keller of the Christophers and Father Patrick Peyton of the Rosary Crusade used mass communication techniques to reach millions of the faithful, but it was Bishop Fulton J. Sheen who epitomized this contemporary devotion to Catholicism. His television show "Life is Worth Living" ran in prime time in the 1950s and attracted an audience of thirty million Americans each week. (*See Reading No. 30.*) It seems that many young Catholics wanted more than a nice house, a new car, and other material goods; they also sought spiritual well-being.

Yet for all this concern about being good Christians, most Catholics were oblivious to the two groups of Catholics who were systematically excluded from the move to the suburbs. Indeed, young Catholics were unwilling to accept, let alone welcome, the growing number of black and Hispanic Catholics into their midst. These latter groups were given the hand-me-down inner-city neighborhoods and parishes abandoned by the whites as they fled to the suburbs. A few bishops—most notably Joseph Ritter of St. Louis and Patrick O'Boyle of Washington—mounted successful campaigns to integrate their diocesan school systems, and Robert E. Lucey of San Antonio led a national social justice crusade to relieve the plight of Hispanic Catholics. However, these were isolated cases; for

*Jay P. Dolan, *The American Catholic Experience: From Colonial Times to the Present* (Garden City, NY, 1985) p. 382.

the most part, the majority of Catholics were either hostile or oblivious to the concerns of black and brown Catholics during the post war years.

Given the racial prejudice in this country during the interwar years it is not surprising that black Catholics were not received warmly into the Church by white Catholics. Blacks were segregated into their own parishes, hidden from view, and restricted in their participation in the life of the Church. At first, the number of black Catholics was small, confined primarily to the South. As factory jobs in northern cities became available, black Catholics joined the great migration north. As their numbers increased, the number of black parishes also increased. In New York, Philadelphia, Chicago, and other large cities, the story was the same. White Catholics fled from their black co-religionists and parishes founded a century earlier by poor immigrants were transferred to poor blacks.

Blacks were not alone as outcasts within the Catholic Church. The arrival of millions of Hispanic Catholics—Mexicans in the southwestern and western states and Puerto Ricans in New York and other eastern cities—presented the Church leadership with yet another challenge. Unlike other ethnic groups, however, Hispanic Catholics considered themselves members of the Church even though they did not attend Mass every week. Their religion was family centered and Hispanics emphasized the importance of those sacraments that supported the family—baptism, marriage, and the last rites. Unlike black Catholics who were eager for integration, Hispanic Catholics would have none of it. They wished to practice Catholicism in their own way.

CATHOLIC EDUCATION. Catholic education presented a major crisis for the American Church in the years after World War II. Simply stated, Catholic educators were surprised by the growing demand for parochial education. In 1949 Catholic elementary and secondary schools had a combined enrollment of 2.6 million students; by the end of the 1950s, however, the figure had more than doubled to 5.4 million and was still rising. Such rapid, ceaseless growth taxed Catholic resources mightily, as Catholic leaders found themselves unprepared to meet the tidal wave of demand.

The rapid growth in Catholic school enrollment quickly became a preoccupation of a new generation of bishops. In virtually every diocese across the nation, bishops and other Catholic leaders built dozens of new schools in the 1950s. In each of the major archdioceses of New York, Boston, Philadelphia, Chicago, and St. Louis, the number of new schools built during the decade climbed into the hundreds. Yet, for all their efforts, these bishops could not build and staff enough schools to meet the demand.

The inability of Church leaders to marshal the funds to build enough classrooms was only part of the problem. Even if they had been able to provide a desk for every child who wanted to attend, there were not enough Catholic teachers to staff all of the classrooms. The continuing lack of competent teachers was the critical weakness of parochial education in the postwar years. For more than a century Catholic leaders had depended on poorly-paid nuns to staff their classrooms, but beginning in the late 1940s there was an increasing shortage of teaching sisters. To fill the gap Catholic educators became more dependent on lay teachers.

The short-term boom in parochial education caused many educators and social commentators to take a critical look at the impact of Catholic schooling on American society. Critic Paul Blanshard and other skeptics argued that parochial schools were divisive—a negative influence on American society—and these critics were not alone. A major public opinion survey conducted in the mid-1950s revealed that a great many Americans were concerned about the negative impact of Catholic schools.

Questions about the effect of parochial education also intrigued social scientists. Working separately in the mid-1950s, Joseph Fichter and Gerhard Lenski conducted sociological studies of parochial education.* Fichter found that Catholic school students were similar to public school students in values and achievement; differences could be found only in the area of social consciousness. Catholic students seemed to be

*Joseph H. Fichter, *Parochial School: A Sociological Study* (Notre Dame, 1958); Gerhard Lenski, *The Religious Factor* (Garden City, NY, 1958).

more concerned about issues such as foreign aid, food and housing for the poor, integration, and anti-Semitism. Reinforcing many of Fichter's findings, Lenski also found that parochial schools were an effective means of sustaining Catholic religious values, and that children who attended parochial schools were more likely to remain loyal and active Catholics than those who attended public schools.

The Fichter and Lenski studies were important first steps in an effort to answer systematically and scientifically some of the fundamental questions and concerns about parochial education. Even though both studies were criticized on methodological grounds, they did make positive contributions to the ongoing debate about the nature of parochial education. These two dissimilar studies had come to the same conclusion that Catholic schools were not a divisive force in American society.

Parochial schooling was not the only concern of Catholic educators. The boom in Catholic education also extended to the colleges and universities. "The massive influx of G.I.s who chose to attend Catholic colleges and universities permanently changed the style of virtually all those institutions," wrote historian James Hennesey in his book, *American Catholics*.* The distinctive parochial identity of many Catholic colleges was gradually replaced by a more secular emphasis on research and teaching. Governmental grants and subsidies further encouraged and later required secularization. By 1960 many Catholic colleges had become sufficiently secular to attract large numbers of non-Catholic students.

Perhaps the biggest change in Catholic higher education came in the graduate programs. Before World War II, virtually all Catholic colleges and universities were devoted to undergraduate education. There were a few Catholic professional schools in medicine, law, business, and dentistry, but little evidence of research or scholarship in the sciences and the humanities. After the war, a number of Catholic universities—Notre Dame and Georgetown among others—began major efforts to expand, increase, and improve their faculties and

*James Hennesey, *American Catholics*, p. 283.

their research and graduate programs. Many of the new faculty members came from war-ravaged Europe, giving these Catholic campuses a distinctly cosmopolitan air.

And yet, for all it growth and expansion in the twentieth century, Catholic colleges and universities had produced only a handful of scholars and intellectuals. "Where are all the Catholic Salks, Oppenheimers, and Einsteins," wondered more than one Catholic educator. This was not a new issue in the postwar years; both Catholics and non-Catholics had been criticizing Catholic colleges and universities for their complacency and mediocrity since the 1920s, but these comments failed to elicit much of a response from the Church establishment.

As this criticism became more common, Catholics became more sensitive to the charge of anti-intellectualism. By 1955, when Father John Tracy Ellis of the Catholic University of America published a harsh assessment of Catholic intellectual life, he touched a nerve. Ellis pointed to the lack of an intellectual tradition in Catholic culture; there was no love of learning for its own sake. "His tone was that of a committed churchman," notes James Hennesey, "his analysis telling and devastating."* (*See Reading No. 31.*) Ellis was joined by a chorus of Catholic academics who committed themselves to improving the intellectual quality of Catholic higher education as well as increasing enrollments.

CATHOLIC–PROTESTANT CONFLICT. The traditional suspicion and hostility between Catholics and Protestants that had been ongoing for more than a century continued into the postwar years. (*See Reading No. 29.*) The violence and overt anti-Catholicism of past decades was gone, but the vitriolic rhetoric on both sides continued to generate more heat than light. The arguments during the postwar years focused on three issues—the continuing appointment of a U.S. ambassador to the Vatican, the effort of Catholics to obtain public funds for parochial schools, and the organized Protestant response to the emerging Catholic influence in American public affairs.

*James Hennesey, *American Catholics*, p. 301.

The initial appointment of a representative to the Vatican had been made by Franklin D. Roosevelt in 1939 on the grounds that such a representative could gather important information that would help the war effort. But in April 1945, President Harry Truman did the unexpected by reappointing Myron Taylor to the Vatican and did the unthinkable a year later when he formally elevated Taylor to the rank of ambassador. Virtually every Protestant denomination responded in opposition. In June 1946, a delegation representing thirty million Protestants met with Truman to tell him that such an appointment was contrary to the American tradition of separating church and state. Truman responded by stating that the appointment was temporary and would end when world peace had been realized.

Yet Truman found the presence of an ambassador at the Vatican to be useful long after the end of hostilities. When Taylor resigned his post in 1950, Truman submitted the name of General Mark Clark for the post. The uproar from the Protestant community and the Senate was so great that Clark asked the President to withdraw the nomination. Truman thought better of making a second nomination and the post remained vacant for another thirty years. American Catholics—particularly the hierarchy—were bitterly disappointed.

In the midst of the controversy over United States–Vatican relations was a conflict over public aid to parochial schools. The opening round came in 1947 when the U.S. Supreme Court, in *Everson v. Board of Education,* permitted school districts to provide free bus transportation to parochial as well as public school students. In approving this aid, the Court was extremely careful to limit the application of its decision. Public aid to parochial schools was constitutional only in very limited circumstances.

The *Everson* decision exacerbated the existing tension between Catholics and Protestants over education. Matters were not helped by Catholic efforts to obtain federal aid for parish schools or by the vitriolic rhetoric of the nation's leading Catholic bishop, Francis Cardinal Spellman of New York. Spellman, for example, accused the *Everson* critics of preaching a crusade against the Catholic Church as an institution, and these accusations aroused the ire of many Protestant leaders who reflected the anxiety of millions of Americans over the political activities of the Catholic hierarchy. Recriminations accomplished nothing and both sides had the good sense to allow the matter to die in the summer of 1947.

The tension did not abate and in May 1949 a bill to provide federal aid to public schools was vigorously opposed by Church leaders. Their anger was due, in part, to a gratuitous provision of the bill prohibiting the states from using any portion of the funds to provide bus transportation for parochial school students as permitted in the *Everson* decision. Cardinal Spellman magnified the dispute by attacking all supporters of the bill, including Eleanor Roosevelt. In fact, Spellman went so far as to accuse the former First Lady of "a record of anti-Catholicism [that] stands for all to see . . . documents of discrimination unworthy of an American mother!" Spellman later muted his criticism in a "clarifying statement," but he did more harm than good in defending parochial education.

The strain between Catholics and Protestants also was intensified during the late 1940s and early 1950s by the establishment of a church-state organization with anti-Catholic overtones. Formed in November 1947, the Protestants and Other Americans United for the Separation of Church and State, opposed any public aid to parochial schools and called for an end to the diplomatic ties with the Vatican. The POAU proclaimed that its goal was "to enlighten and mobilize public opinion in support of religious liberty." Legislative petitions and court action by the POAU were thinly veiled attacks on the Catholic Church.

The POAU did not represent mainstream Protestant opinion of Catholicism. In spite of serious disagreements with various Catholic positions, a number of Protestant groups sought a rapprochement with Catholicism during the latter 1950s. Efforts by the POAU to rally other Protestants around minor issues, such as whether American Catholic cardinals could vote in papal elections, were met with derision. By the end of the 1950s the POAU no longer was a force in interfaith relations. Catholics and Protestants had come to accept and tolerate their respective rights in a pluralistic American society.

CATHOLICISM AND AMERICAN POLITICS. The
fifteen years from 1945 to 1960 were a time of unprecedented
political activity for American Catholics. Moreover, Catholicism and Catholic patriotism were highly visible in American
political debates during those years. The focal points of these
debates were two Catholic U.S. senators—Joseph R. Mc-
Carthy of Wisconsin and John F. Kennedy of Massachusetts.
The former came to prominence as a crusader against communism, but was later exposed as a manipulator who had no
respect for civil liberties. The latter was a cautious, calculat-
ing politician who succeeded in doing what many Americans
thought was impossible for a Catholic—getting elected President of the United States. The stories of these two men under-
score the relationship between Catholicism and American politics during those years.

Anticommunism had been a Catholic tradition long before
the appearance of Joe McCarthy. The Church had always been
hostile to a system of governance that considered religion to
be ''the opiate of the people,'' but postwar concern over the
Soviet Union expanded Catholic efforts to fight communism,
particularly within American society. It was McCarthy, a
Catholic war veteran elected to the Senate in 1946, who would
turn anticommunism into a Catholic crusade.

McCarthy wrapped himself in the American flag and made
unsubstantiated charges regarding a Communist influence
within the federal government. He used congressional hearings
to harass and abuse Americans of all political persuasions and
cared not for the truth of the matters he was investigating. The
fact that such a man could be embraced as a hero is evidence
of the extent of the irrational American fear of communism
during those years. McCarthy went too far when he revealed
himself to be a bully during televised congressional hearings in
1954. The Senate eventually censured him for his outrageous
behavior and he suffered an ignominious death in 1957.

Given the anti-Communist impulse of American Catholics,
and McCarthy's emergence as the leading anti-Communist in
the nation, it is reasonable to assume that Catholics were united
in their support for the senator from Wisconsin. Indeed, almost
every contemporary political commentator proclaimed this assumption as fact. To be sure, Catholics did support McCarthy

in large numbers and in percentages greater than the American public in general, but the Catholic support for McCarthy was far from unanimous. In fact, liberal bishops such as Bernard J. Sheil of Chicago repudiated McCarthy, and most Catholics, while remaining anti-Communist, rejected his outrageous tactics.

One of the strongest centers of support for McCarthy was the state of Massachusetts. The junior senator from the state, John F. Kennedy, was careful not to offend his constituents by criticizing McCarthy, but he did nothing to support his Catholic senatorial colleague. Like many Catholics throughout the country, Kennedy ignored McCarthy altogether. The senator from Massachusetts had bigger plans on his mind.

Kennedy and his family set the presidency as a goal sometime in the mid-1950s. Some historians trace the Kennedy family's presidential ambitions back to Joseph Kennedy, Jr., the older brother who died in World War II. Whatever the case, John Kennedy burst on to the national political scene with a strong bid for the vice-presidential nomination at the Democratic national convention of 1956. His impressive showing at the convention made him someone to be watched and, as was his plan, the senator took advantage of all the media attention.

Kennedy began running for the presidency in earnest shortly after Dwight Eisenhower was reelected in 1956. As might be expected, the senator was dogged by the question of whether a Catholic could serve as President. Because this issue had been the downfall of Al Smith in 1928, Kennedy took it very seriously. He used many speaking opportunities to stress his belief in the separation of church and state, his opposition to diplomatic relations with the Vatican, and his opposition to public aid for parochial schools. Although these positions alienated some Catholic voters, many Protestants were won over to the young senator from Massachusetts.

The religion issue dogged Kennedy in the political primaries during the Spring of 1960. Could Kennedy win enough delegates to take the nomination? Would non-Catholic Democrats support him? A major test came in the Democratic primary in West Virginia where Catholics constituted only five percent of the population. To neutralize the religious issue, Kennedy solicited the support of major Protestant leaders in the preparation of a letter on religious tolerance. Religion should not be part of the campaign noted the letter which was sent to every Protestant minister in West Virginia. The letter may have helped as Kennedy won a strong sixty-one percent of the vote. With this stunning victory, Kennedy hoped that the religion issue was behind him.

After winning the Democratic nomination in July, Kennedy girded for more questions about his Catholicism. To address the religious issues, the candidate enlisted James Wine, former associate general secretary of the National Council of Churches and John Cogley, a former editor of the Catholic journal, *The Commonweal*. Wine and Cogley devoted their time to combating rumors and innuendo about Kennedy and his beliefs. The candidate was willing to speak openly about his religion and its relationship to the presidency.

The religion issue came to a climax in September with the formation of the ''National Conference of Citizens for Religious Freedom,'' a group actively opposed to Kennedy because of his Catholicism. Among the leaders of the group were notables such as Norman Vincent Peale, the editors of two major Protestant periodicals, the head of the National Association of Evangelicals, and the leadership of the POAU. The anti-Catholic and anti-Kennedy efforts of the group were countered by the voices of a number of other Protestant and Jewish clergymen including Reinhold Niebuhr, John Bennett, and Arthur Hertzberg.

Kennedy, himself, chose to address the religion issue for the final time on September 12, in an address to the Greater Houston Ministerial Association. Once again, he emphasized his commitment to the absolute separation of church and state—''where no Catholic prelate would tell the President (should he be a Catholic) how to act, and no Protestant minister would tell his parishioners for whom to vote.'' It was a masterful speech that largely ended the concerns about Kennedy's Catholicism. (*See Reading No. 33.*)

It is not possible to determine what was the critical factor in helping Kennedy to win one of the closest elections in American history. It seems clear, however, that religion was not that critical factor. To be sure, Catholics voted for Kennedy in overwhelming numbers—George Gallup estimated that seventy-eight percent of them had voted for Kennedy in 1960. Yet Kennedy was not elected by his fellow Catholics, but by a coalition of traditional Democratic voters. Blacks, Jews, and working-class Protestants also supported the Democratic candidate in large numbers, and Kennedy was responsive to their needs. It was Kennedy's ability to transcend the issue of his religion that won him 34.1 million votes, more than twice the votes that Al Smith received in 1928. It was a significant victory for all Americans who believed in religious toleration.

CONCLUSION. The postwar years saw the ultimate end to the barriers that had separated Catholics from one another and from other Americans. Young Catholics had fought side by side with other Americans during the war; they saw no reason to separate themselves from the rest of society after the war because of their religion. Also, these young Catholics cared far less about the ethnic heritage that was so important to their parents and grandparents. Perhaps the most dramatic evidence of that fact was the sharp increase in the percentage of interethnic Catholic marriages in the 1940s and 1950s.

This is not to say that the barriers between Catholics and other Americans had disappeared completely. During the late 1940s and 1950s, Catholics held controversial positions on federal aid to parochial schools and United States representation at the Vatican. These issues generated some heated debate between Catholics and non-Catholics in the pages of both the secular and religious press.

This state of affairs would be changed by the middle of the 1950s when Catholics established a dialogue with American Protestants that continues to the present day. (*See Reading No. 32.*) The election of Pope John XXIII, beloved by non-Catholics as well as Catholics, and the announcement of an ecumenical council to reevaluate the role of the Church in the modern world, helped to facilitate this dialogue. Certainly the most dramatic evidence of the improved relations between Catholics and Protestants during these years was the willingness of Protestants and other Americans to join with Catholics in electing John F. Kennedy as president of the United States. There no longer seemed to be dichotomy between Catholicism and American values.

CHAPTER 9

THE AMERICAN CATHOLIC
REVOLUTION, 1960–1980

By 1960 Catholics had achieved an unprecedented status in American society. Sociological surveys, public opinion polls, and demographic studies all confirmed that American Catholics were better educated, better employed, and held more liberal social attitudes than the American population as a whole.* The election of John F. Kennedy as President was the apex of the extraordinary progress that the Catholic community had made since 1634.

Even bigger changes in American Catholicism were yet to come, the result of a religious council held outside the United States. The changes in Church liturgy and doctrine promulgated by the Second Vatican Council (1962–1965) gave birth to a revolution in American Catholicism that would last for the next decade and beyond. Vocations to the priesthood and the religious life would decline precipitously, enrollments in Catholic schools would drop by half, and lay people would become intimately involved in the operation of parishes and dioceses across the nation. More important, American Catholics—priests and nuns as well as laity—would begin to follow their own consciences on personal matters such as birth control, abortion, and divorce. American Catholicism would lose the bond of discipline and uniformity that had distinguished it from other denominations during the middle years of the twentieth century.

THE SECOND VATICAN COUNCIL. The event most directly responsible for the turmoil within the American

---

*The majority of these studies were conducted by the National Opinion Research Center at the University of Chicago; additional polls and surveys were conducted by the George Gallup and Lou Harris organizations. See Jay P. Dolan, *The American Catholic Experience,* p. 426 and Thomas J. Archdeacon, *Becoming American: An Ethnic History,* (New York, 1983) p. 222.

Church was the Second Vatican Council. When he convened the first international council of Catholic bishops in nearly a century, Pope John XXIII talked about opening the windows and letting a little fresh air into the Church. Indeed, the Council did more than that as the bishops of the world revised and changed Church policy and law on the liturgy, ecumenism, the religious life, and religious liberty among other aspects of Catholicism.

The American Catholic bishops were among the most active participants in the Council. Although they played a role in promulgating many decrees, it was the declaration on religious liberty that was of greatest importance to the American bishops. The passage of the decrees had been a struggle because many conservative European bishops believed that a decree recognizing the religious rights of non-Catholics legitimized the Protestant Reformation. The American bishops, nevertheless, were united in their view that a person's right to religious freedom was based on Catholic principles and constituted a "pastoral necessity of the first order." (*See Reading No. 34.*) In the end, nearly 2,000 of the 2,200 bishops present voted for the decree.

As important as the religious liberty decree was, it had far less impact on the lives of American Catholics than the decree on the liturgy. For most American Catholics, the impact of Vatican II was seen most dramatically in the celebration of the Mass. Before the Council, priests said the Mass in Latin facing an altar at the back of the sanctuary of the church. The laity played only a limited role in the liturgy, for the most part observing the priest and praying in silence. But Vatican II changed all that. By the end of the 1960s the Mass was said in English at an altar facing the congregation. The laity was called upon to sing, pray aloud, extend a handshake of peace to one another, read to the congregation, and even to distribute communion.

Although American Catholics accepted these changes without comment, many conservative Catholics were disgruntled by the new liturgy. "We don't feel holy when we go to church anymore," noted one unhappy Catholic. "Not everything is different. But we don't feel comfortable, and it just don't seem right if you know what I mean." A number of pastors and bishops felt equally uncomfortable, and these traditionalists slowed the impact of Vatican II in scattered parishes and dioceses.

There was no turning back, however. The liturgical changes set off a chain reaction. Pre-Vatican II liturgies such as missions, Marian devotions, and novenas disappeared from many parishes. Mass became less ritualistic and ceremonial and was often celebrated in informal settings outside of churches. Blacks and Hispanics adapted their cultural traditions to the new Catholic liturgy and thousands of Catholics parishes across the country participated in spiritual renewal programs. Liturgical experimentation was commonplace.

Perhaps the most extraordinary liturgical development was the charismatic movement. Influenced by Protestant pentacostalism and the intense spiritual retreats of the Cursillo movement, a small group of Catholics organized highly emotional retreats and prayer meetings for Catholics in the late 1960s. The movement caught on slowly at first and was viewed with suspicion by many. By the 1980s, there were more than 5,700 charismatic prayer groups in the United States alone; these groups attracted an estimated 500,000 Catholics each week to their meetings. One scholar estimates that since it began in 1967, the charismatic movement has touched the lives of eight to ten million Catholics.

Yet it was not the laity that was most directly affected by Vatican II, it was priests and nuns. The Second Vatican Council in its decrees on the priestly ministry and the religious life called upon priests and women religious to reexamine their roles in contemporary society. The end result was that many individuals abandoned the religious life as irrelevant. One scholar estimates that ten thousand men left the priesthood in the twelve years following the Council. The shortage of priests was worsened by a general decline in the number of young men entering seminaries to study for the priesthood. In 1964, for example, there were almost 50,000 seminarians, but by the 1980s, enrollments had dropped to 12,000.

The circumstances were largely the same for women religious. There was a steady decline in the number of sisters from a high of 180,000 in 1966 to fewer than 120,000 in the 1980s for several reasons. Certainly the decrease in the number of young women entering the convent was a major factor. As older nuns died, there were fewer young ones to take their place. Just as important, however, was the substantial number of women who left the convent to pursue other concerns. Some women no longer found fulfillment in the religious life; others were frustrated at the slow pace of change within their religious orders. Whatever the reason, Vatican II set off a sustained decline in the number of available women religious for service in schools, hospitals, asylums, and other Catholic social institutions.

Vatican II also set off a change in Catholic attitudes on controversial subjects such as birth control and divorce. The Council seemed to free Catholics from the bonds of guilt and deference to clerical authority. Before Vatican II, lay Catholics generally followed the lead of their pastors on all spiritual and moral matters; in fact, many Catholics were proud of the rigorous discipline of their religion. After Vatican II, however, Catholics felt free to question the pronouncements of their priests, their bishops, and even their Pope. This lay Catholic independence was documented most dramatically in the general rejection of Pope Paul VI's 1968 encyclical, *Humanae Vitae,* calling for an end to the use of artificial contraception. (*See Reading No. 35.*)

Catholics also pushed for a revision in the Church's attitude toward annulments and divorce and many priests and bishops were sympathetic. In 1967 there were about 700 annulments granted annually in the United States; by 1977, the number had jumped to 25,000. Many American Catholics were questioning Church doctrine for the first time.

CATHOLIC EDUCATION. Vatican II also had a significant impact on parochial education in the United States. The Council had precipitated an identity crisis among many of the women religious who staffed parochial classrooms and it also caused Catholic parents to question the value and purpose of Catholic schools. When a New Hampshire housewife named Mary Perkins Ryan published *Are Catholic Schools the Answer?* in 1964, a national debate ensued. In light of Vatican II, Ryan argued that the Church should use the considerable resources expended on the parochial schools for other, more important ministries. Although the book was widely criticized and the value of Catholic education defended, Ryan reflected the doubts that many Catholics felt about the long-term value and purpose of their schools.

These doubts were manifest in a steady decline in enrollments and a rise in school closings. During the two decades following Vatican II, 27 percent of the Catholic parochial schools and 40 percent of the Catholic high schools in the United States closed their doors. Enrollments had risen 162 percent in the years from 1945 to 1962, but each year after 1965 saw a marked decrease in the numbers. Total enrollment dropped from a high of 5.6 million students in 1965 to a little more than 3 million in the 1980s. The long-term decline was so evident by 1970 that William Brown and Andrew Greeley published a little book with a big title. *Can Catholic Schools Survive?*, they asked. "Yes" was their answer and that of other educators, but not in its pre-Council form.

In the midst of this downturn, many Catholic educators re-emphasized the substantive value of parochial education. Survival, they noted, took only the commitment of the parents to sustain the schools. (*See Reading No. 37.*) The most valiant case studies of parochial school survival were to be found in the inner-city parishes of major archdioceses. Poor working-class parents, fearful of the violence so prevalent in inner-city public schools, took second and third jobs to pay tuition for their children at local parochial schools. Many of these parents were not Catholic, but their commitment to parochial schools was no less than that of Catholic parents. Many in the ghetto—regardless of religion—agreed that parochial schools provided an important alternative to public education.

The rapid and sustained changes in parochial education during the 1960s and 1970s were matched by changes in higher education. Catholic colleges and universities faced two major issues in the 1960s. Academic freedom was the first issue that led to conflict on several Catholic campuses as faculty and students took controversial positions on moral and social issues, often in opposition to the Church hierarchy. More than any other institution, it was the Catholic University of America that was the focal point for these conflicts. Efforts to ban or fire controversial theologians such as John Courtney Murray, Gustave Weigel, and Charles Curran caused many educators to question the survival of academic freedom at Catholic University specifically and at Catholic colleges generally.

The second issue was more subtle, but also more sweeping. Catholic higher education suffered an identity crisis in the years after Vatican II. What was the new mission of Catholic higher education? Many Catholic colleges searched for the ways and means to be distinctive in an increasingly secular society. To be sure, these Catholic colleges committed themselves to excellence in teaching and research in the arts and sciences, but there needed to be more to higher education. Many Catholic colleges and universities established new theology and social justice programs that emphasized the moral fabric of Catholic higher education. Yet no completely satisfactory answer has been found and many Catholic colleges continued to reexamine their purpose into the 1980s.

SOCIAL JUSTICE AND PROTEST. The 1960s and 1970s were a time of increased social consciousness for all Americans, and Catholics were swept up in this movement. Millions of American Catholics recommitted themselves to the gospel message of doing unto others as they wanted others to do unto them. Virtually every social justice campaign during these two decades contained a large contingent of Catholics— priests, nuns, and even a few bishops as well as the laity. Yet not every Catholic supported these campaigns and many traditionalists resented what they saw as a radical turn in their once conservative, stolid Church.

The plight of the Chicano farm workers of the Southwest was a focal point of Catholic concern. For generations, Mexican-Americans had worked in the fields of California and other states with little to show for their efforts. These impoverished Catholic immigrants had no spokesman to defend them and argue for their rights. A man named Caesar Chavez changed all that. With the assistance of Father Donald McDowell and labor organizer Fred Ross, Chavez established the National Farm Workers Organization which worked tirelessly for the rights of the field hands. It was a deeply religious effort with the Mass featured as an important part of many protests. Thousands of Catholics joined *la causa* and millions more

THE AMERICAN CATHOLIC REVOLUTION, 1960–1980

participated in the grape and lettuce boycotts that led to union contracts for farm workers.

Catholics also were involved in the civil rights movement. The poverty, racism, and injustice faced by black Americans had been a growing concern of Catholics during the 1950s. When the Reverend Martin Luther King, Jr., galvanized the civil rights movement in the early 1960s, tens of thousands of Catholics followed his call. Thousands of priests and nuns were in the crowd in Washington in 1963 to hear King tell of his dream; hundreds more marched with him at Selma, Alabama two years later. In 1966 King took his campaign north to cities like Chicago and Milwaukee to lead the protest against segregated housing and job discrimination, and once again he was joined by Catholics. Some of those who resisted King's marches also were Catholics. The social justice movement acquired a solid institutional base within the Catholic Church in the late 1960s, as programs such as the Catholic Committee on Urban Ministry solidified the Catholic effort to address social justice issues on the local and diocesan levels. The national Campaign for Human Development started in 1970 under the aegis of the U.S. Catholic Conference; it raised over 75 million dollars during the 1970s for 1500 projects to help the poor and oppressed.

The foremost issue of the 1960s was the Vietnam War. It divided communities, churches, and families. Conservatives proclaimed America's right to help the South Vietnamese defend themselves against northern aggressors. Liberals refuted this claim by arguing that the Americans were the aggressors, defending a corrupt South Vietnamese government.

Catholicism was as badly divided on Vietnam as any other denomination. On the conservative side was Cardinal Francis Spellman who visited the troops in Vietnam and defended "our country, right or wrong." On the other side were Daniel and Philip Berrigan, brother priests who led numerous protests and acts of civil disobedience against the war.

American Catholic opinion on the war changed with that of the general populace. In the mid-1960s, most Catholics—including the bishops—were loyal supporters of the war effort, but by 1968, almost everyone harbored doubts and the bishops issued a pastoral letter defending the principle of Catholic conscientious objection. That same year the Berrigan brothers burned draft files at Catonsville, Maryland and their trial became a national forum on the morality of the selective service law. (*See Reading No. 36.*) By 1971 a great many Catholics had turned against the war, a reflection of the growing disenhancement with American policy in Vietnam on the part of the American people.

NATIONAL CHURCH LEADERSHIP. A final point of friction in the 1960s and 1970s was leadership and decision making within the Church. A major shift in power took place during those years, a change brought on by two factors. First, an older, somewhat autocratic generation of bishops had passed on by 1970. Men such as John O'Hara of Philadelphia, Samuel Stritch of Chicago, Francis Spellman of New York, Richard Cushing of Boston, Edward Mooney of Detroit, and Joseph Ritter of St. Louis had risen to leadership within the Church at a time when bishops made decisions unilaterally, rarely consulting with priests, religious, and laity. Their replacements were men who were generally more sensitive to the needs of various interest groups within the Church. This new generation of bishops was more willing to share power.

The major impetus for change in the leadership of American Catholicism was the Second Vatican Council. The Council criticized the lack of participation and dialogue within the Church, and suggested that collegiality should replace autocracy as the model for decision making at all levels. The Pope was to consult with his fellow bishops; bishops were to consult with each other, with their priests, nuns and the laity; and pastors were to consult with each other and with the nuns and lay people in their parishes.

This call for collegiality precipitated a new wave of national organizations within the American Church. The bishops took the lead by transforming the National Catholic Welfare Conference into a two-part organization: The National Conference of Catholic Bishops and the United States Catholic Conference. The NCCB was the national decision-making body of the bishops; the USCC was the administrative agency that implemented NCCB policy. The new structure provided for annual meetings of all the bishops to discuss both pastoral and administrative issues facing the American Church.

Priests, religious, and laity also established national organizations. The National Federation of Priest Councils, the National Coalition of American Nuns and the National Association of Catholic Laymen were established in the late 1960s to give new organizational voices to these major groups within the Church. Existing organizations such as the Leadership Conference of Women Religious and Conference of Superiors of Major Orders of Men also took on new visibility during these years. New groups within the Church—Hispanics and blacks in particular—also established national organizations. The renewal and expansion of the concept of collegiality was a return to traditions of the Councils of Baltimore and it was widely applauded by American Catholics.

Leadership on the diocesan level varied substantially depending on the views of the local bishop. Some conservative bishops did little to involve priests, religious, and laity in diocesan decision making. Priests who objected to ecclesial authority found themselves assigned to the least desirable parishes; religious orders that objected to the bishop's orders were dismissed from the diocese. Yet the majority of bishops embraced the concept of collegiality and actively promoted dialogues with priests, religious, and laity. "We, bishop and pastors," noted one bishop to his flock, "are to serve your needs; our service must be to let you exercise your freedom as sons of God."

Certainly the greatest changes in leadership in the years after Vatican II came on the local level. Before 1965, the pastor was the sole and exclusive leader of the parish. All the decisions on liturgy, education, finances, and other matters were made by the pastor, but the establishment of parish councils in the late 1960s precipitated a shift in decision making. To be sure, parish government did not become democratic; the pastor remained the final authority. The Council, however, gave lay people a voice in parish affairs for the first time since the trustee movement almost two centuries earlier.

By 1980, lay involvement was evident in every aspect of parish life. Lay people were participating in the liturgy as deacons, extraordinary ministers of the Eucharist, and as lectors. They were serving as directors of religious education and were supervising parish finances. Women, in particular, assumed important leadership positions in the American Catholic parish. A recent study of parish life notes that lay people "discovered that by doing the many ministries of the parish, they had a pervasive effect on the life of the parish."*

A final aspect of the transformation of post–Vatican II leadership was the involvement of priests and nuns in the public sector. If the election of John F. Kennedy encouraged other Catholic laymen to run for office, Vatican II had a similar effect on those in the religious life. Thus, in the 1970s, the Roman collar could be found in the halls of state capitals and even on the floor of the U.S. Congress. Among the more notable religious who held public office in the 1960s and 1970s were Theodore M. Hesburgh, C.S.C., who served as Chairman of the U.S. Civil Rights Commission; Robert Cornell, O. Praem. and Robert Drinan, S.J., who served as Members of Congress; and Geno Baroni, who was an Assistant Secretary of Housing and Urban Development. This involvement in public life came to an end for most religious in 1980 when Pope John Paul II called for priests and nuns to recommit themselves to the religious life and leave politics to the laity.

CONCLUSION. The 1960s and 1970s marked a major upheaval in American Catholicism. Since the foundation of the nation, American Catholics had been concerned about loyalty to both their religion and their country. Catholics were both devoted followers of papal authority and flag-waving American patriots, but the election of John F. Kennedy and the work of the Vatican Council helped Catholics to shed the last vestiges of their inferiority complex. In the 1960s and 1970s, American Catholics felt free to question the politics of both their Church and their country.

The result was nothing short of revolutionary. Catholics at

*Jay P. Dolan and David C. Leege, "A Profile of American Catholic Parishes and Parishioners: 1820s to 1980s," *Notre Dame Study of Catholic Parish Life*, Report No. 2, (February 1985) p. 4.

all levels of the American Church began to make decisions for themselves. Birth control, divorce, premarital sex, all became matters of personal conscience. Catholics also demanded to participate in making the decisions that affected both their secular and religious worlds. They joined social action groups, ran for political office, protested in the streets, served on parish councils, and became involved in a wide variety of causes, both liberal and conservative.

By 1980, American Catholics were on every side of every issue, uncertain about the future direction of their religion. They looked to a new, charismatic Pope to provide direction to an American Catholic world turned upside down. Yet many Catholics were apprehensive about whether Pope John Paul II would lead the American Church into the future or take it back to the past. The 1980s would be consumed by this concern.

CHAPTER 10

TOWARD A NEW CENTURY

The visit of Pope John Paul II to the United States in October 1979 was a joyous occasion for American Catholicism. John Paul was a relatively young, vigorous, charismatic leader—the first non-Italian to be elected Pope in over four centuries! His visit attracted millions of Americans, Catholic and non-Catholic, curious to see what this new man was like. Hundreds of thousands of people waited at each stop—Boston, New York, Philadelphia, Chicago, Des Moines, and Washington—to celebrate the Mass with the new Pope and hear him speak. Even though many liberals were concerned about John Paul's conservative views on the liturgy, the religious life, and sexuality, most American Catholics had high hopes that he would come to understand and appreciate the special faith of his American flock. In the afterglow of this papal visit, American Catholics appeared to be at peace with one another and full of new optimism for the future.

The impact of the papal visit proved to be cosmetic. The two decades of revolution since 1960 had precipitated issues and problems that could not be solved by a brief visit from the new Pope, no matter how charismatic. During the 1980s, therefore, American Catholics continued to struggle with many of the issues of the previous two decades—papal authority, episcopal leadership, and the changing shape of Catholic parish life. American Catholics fought with one another and with Rome over how to address these issues. When the Pope again visited the United States in September 1987, controversy and protest dogged his every step.

PAPAL AUTHORITY. No issue divided American Catholics during the 1980s more than the issue of papal authority. This is not to say that anyone challenged the role of the Pope as head of the Catholic Church; even the most independent-minded Catholics acknowledged the Pope as their spiritual leader, but beyond that basic agreement, there were many questions. (*See Reading No. 40.*) How much influence should

101

the Vatican have in American Church affairs? Should the papacy establish standards of orthodoxy and demand that all Catholics conform? How much freedom should be given to bishops to lead their dioceses as they see fit? How much freedom should be given to Catholic theologians and universities to explore controversial issues?

These questions accentuated the growing factionalism in American Catholicism. On the right were conservatives who stood firmly behind the Pope and conducted letter-writing campaigns against bishops, theologians, and others who, in their opinion, had strayed from the one true way of the Church. On the left were the liberals who chafed at the notion of any Vatican involvement in American Church affairs. American Catholicism in the 1980s has become known for its divisions rather than its commonality.

Unquestionably, this internecine warfare in American Catholicism has caused anxiety in the Vatican. Each week the Pope and various Vatican officials receive letters of complaint about the state of American Catholicism. To be sure, most of these letters have been written by a small number of conservative Catholics upset about the general course of American Catholicism since Vatican II. But the Vatican takes these letters seriously because they confirm Rome's worst fear—that the American Church is becoming too independent. "The Roman Curia sees U.S. Catholicism as one of the world's most vibrant Catholic communities," noted one conservative Catholic paper in April 1987, "yet also one of those poised between fidelity to the Catholic tradition and abandonment of central elements of that tradition under the influence of American culture."*

Rome has worked simultaneously on several fronts to assert its authority over American Catholicism. Through pastoral letters and encyclicals, the Pope has stressed the vital importance of the "magisterium"—the traditional teaching authority of the Catholic Church. On *all* matters of faith and morality, for example, the Pope has stressed that all Catholics must follow him with unquestioning fidelity.

---

*Robert Moynihan, "Hope, Unease Shape Roman View of the U.S. Church," *National Catholic Register* (April 19, 1987).

What has been the response in the United States to the Pope's messages? A mixture of respect and rejection. Virtually all American Catholics accept the Pope as their spiritual leader and listen with respect to all that Rome says. On matters such as abortion, homosexuality, and sexual fidelity within marriage, the vast majority of American Catholics agree with the Vatican. But on other issues—contraception, divorce, remarriage, and premarital sex—a significant majority reject what the Pope has said. This is not a new phenomenon; Pope Paul VI was shocked at the overwhelming rejection of his 1968 encyclical on birth control. John Paul continues to struggle with the dilemma of changing the views of millions of independent-minded American Catholics on these issues.

To reassert his authority over American Catholic affairs, the Pope has taken several specific actions. The Vatican has moved against those bishops who have been accused of unorthodox practices. In 1986, for example, the Pope limited the episcopal authority of Archbishop Raymond Hunthausen of Seattle over a number of aspects of diocesan life because of various charges brought by conservatives in the archdiocese. These ecclesial responsibilities were reassigned to a newly appointed auxiliary bishop. Hunthausen was thought by many Vatican officials to be too liberal on matters such as homosexuality, the liturgy, and the religious life. The reassignment of duties seemed to be an efficient and judicious way of reestablishing orthodoxy in Seattle.

The Vatican did not anticipate the outcry of Catholics within the archdiocese and across the nation. The Hunthausen case became the major Catholic news story of the year as reporters and commentators accused the Vatican of heavy-handed, anti-democratic actions. A tension-filled meeting of the American Catholic bishops in November indicated that the Hunthausen case was a matter of national concern. In response, Rome sought to relieve the tension by appointing a small commission of American archbishops to investigate the charges. After due investigation, the commission criticized Hunthausen for certain practices, but recommended restoration of his authority.

The Pope acceded to the commission's recommendations, thereby underscoring the right of the American bishops to resolve their own problems without Vatican interference. But

Rome also made it clear—bishops who wandered too far from orthodoxy would not be tolerated for long. If the American bishops would not discipline their own, the Vatican would step in.

On a second issue related to papal authority, the Vatican saw no need to defer to the American bishops. Over the two decades since the end of Vatican II, Rome had become increasingly concerned about the divergent views of American Catholic theologians on abortion, birth control, premarital sex, and homosexuality. Something had to be done to bring these theologians into line with the official position of the Church.

Two actions were taken in the 1980s to reassert papal authority over American Catholic theologians. First, the Vatican commissioned a study of Catholic seminaries in the United States to make sure that young men preparing for the priesthood were being taught the orthodox Catholic position on moral issues. The seminary study caused some concern, but little controversy; it revealed that American Catholic seminaries were in line with Rome.

Next, the Vatican moved against a prominent moral theologian, Father Charles Curran of the Catholic University of America, by removing his authority to teach Catholic moral theology. The action against Curran has generated pages of comment in the higher education community because of its apparent disregard for academic freedom. As a result of the Vatican action, Curran has been suspended from his teaching position at CUA. He, in turn, has vowed to pursue the case through the university appeal process and the courts if necessary to regain his position. What the Vatican did not anticipate was the outcry of Catholics.

Both the Hunthausen case and the Curran case point to the fact that diversity can be a dangerous word within American Catholicism. "In the view of the Vatican," wrote one reporter, "there appears to be little room for the democratic model or even the loyal opposition; rather authority and direction flow from the top."* It remains to be seen how American

---

*Ari L. Goldman, "Catholicism, Democracy, and the Case of Father Curran," *The New York Times* (August 24, 1986).

Catholics will respond to this new emphasis on papal authority. Public opinion seems to indicate that the fidelity of American Catholics to the pronouncements and actions of the Vatican is decided on a case by case basis.

EPISCOPAL LEADERSHIP. The task of leading the American Church was not any easier in the 1980s than it was in the years immediately after Vatican II. In fact, there are some bishops who would argue that the task has become more difficult with each passing year. In addition to the traditional problems of fund-raising, education, social institutions, vocations, and liturgy, the bishops now worry about the Vatican second-guessing their decisions.

In many ways the Catholic bishops of the 1980s have become prisoners of the management style that made their predecessors so powerful. Beginning in the 1920s, a generation of so-called "consolidating bishops" developed substantial church bureaucracies to administer diocesan affairs. Although the new structure did tighten diocesan control over parish affairs, it did not necessarily enhance the bishop's role as the leader of his diocese. In truth, the bishops were isolated from many diocesan issues because these matters were handled by bureaucratic experts. In cases of finances, charity, building construction, even the assignment of priests, the bishop is always informed, but in many instances does not administer or direct. The question remains open whether the bishops of the twenty-first century will diminish the importance of the bureaucracy and reclaim their roles as leaders.

This is not to say that individual bishops refused to take the lead on issues of importance to their dioceses. A select number of bishops—most notably Cardinals Joseph Bernardin of Chicago and John O'Connor of New York—took strong stands against abortion and later found themselves caught up in controversy. In 1983, for example, Bernardin proposed that Catholics support a "consistent life ethic" by linking opposition to all life-threatening activities. Nuclear warfare, capital punishment, euthanasia, and abortion were points on the same spectrum. Bernardin's position offended both liberals and conservatives who had been selective about their pro-life activities. (*See Reading No. 39.*)

Cardinal O'Connor spoke out to refute the claims of some Catholics that abortion was a matter of personal choice. Catholics could not in good conscience condone and support abortion under any circumstances, O'Connor noted. But his statement, coming as it did in the midst of the 1984 presidential elections, appeared to be a direct criticism of Geraldine Ferraro, the Catholic vice-presidential candidate on the Democratic ticket who considered abortion a matter of personal choice. The controversy was twisted and distorted in the media and did little but polarize voters.

Yet the influence of the American Catholic bishops has been enhanced in the 1980s through their role as teachers. In two recent pastoral letters—one on nuclear war and the other on the economy—the bishops took courageous, if controversial, stands that gave stature to American Catholic thought on these issues. The opinions of the bishops in these letters was by no means reflective of past episcopal pastorals or papal encyclicals. "There were no precedents to invoke," noted Father Theodore Hesburgh of Notre Dame of the pastoral on nuclear weapons, "no history to depend upon for a wise lesson, no real theology except for that which dates back to pacifism or a just-war doctrine in a day of spears, swords, bows and arrows not ICBMS."*

The struggle for the so-called "peace pastoral" has been told at great length. (*See Reading No. 38.*) Over a three-year period from 1980 to 1983 the bishops worked to develop and approve the most powerful and far-reaching statement on the threat of nuclear war. "The arms race is one of the greatest curses on the human race," noted the pastoral in unequivocal terms, "it is to be condemned as a danger, an act of aggression against the poor, and a folly which does not provide the security it promises." Such a statement was very controversial, coming as it did in the midst of the Reagan administration's arms build-up.

Even though American Catholics supported Ronald Reagan in the election campaigns of 1980 and 1984, they also came to

---

*Theodore M. Hesburgh, "Foreword," to Jim Castelli, *The Bishops and the Bomb* (Garden City, NY, 1984).

agree with the bishop's statement on peace. In fact, the National Opinion Research Center at the University of Chicago collected survey data that showed a significant shift in the attitude of Catholics against defense spending in the six months following the publication of the peace pastoral.* The prestige and influence of the bishops as pastors increased substantially as a result of the pastoral.

If the bishops could make an impact on the laity when speaking on matters of war and peace, why have they not had the same impact when speaking on matters such as contraception or women in the Church? The answer is complex. Andrew Greeley, the priest-sociologist, points out that the power of the bishops as teachers is probably limited by their ability to persuade the laity of the righteousness of their views. This was not an easy task. Many Catholics in public office had sworn to uphold laws that were in conflict with Catholic moral values. (*See Reading No. 40.*) Other Catholics listened to the bishops, but chose to follow their consciences instead. In the 1980s, the laity seemed willing to follow the bishops on nuclear war, but not on sexuality.

A second controversial pastoral letter was approved by the bishops at their annual meeting in November 1986. *Economic Justice For All: Catholic Social Teaching and the U.S. Economy* was intended to stimulate "the public debate about the directions in which the U.S. economy should be moving." There is no question that the pastoral achieved that end. The first and second drafts of the pastoral were distributed in 1984 and 1985 and were greeted with both praise and criticism. Indeed, the pastoral seemed to widen the divisions between the liberal and conservative factions of American Catholicism. (*See Reading No. 41.*)

The final draft, as published in 1986, was not ambiguous. "We call for a new national commitment to full employment," the bishops wrote, "We say it is a social and a moral scandal that one of every seven Americans is poor and we call for efforts to eradicate poverty. The fulfillment of the basic

---

*Andrew M. Greeley, *American Catholics Since the Council,* (Chicago, 1985), p. 94.

needs of the poor is of the highest priority.'' Conservatives were so alarmed by what they feared would be the Socialist tone of the pastoral that they formed a lay Catholic commission to prepare a defense of capitalism and rebut the bishops' charges long before their first draft of the letter had been distributed.

It is not likely that the economic pastoral, as it is called, will have the impact of the peace pastoral. Nevertheless, the willingness of the bishops to address controversial issues in unequivocal terms has won the respect and admiration of both Catholics and non-Catholics. These two pastoral letters enhanced the national leadership role of the Catholic bishops in the United States.

PARISH AND RELIGIOUS LIFE. The interest of the media in papal authority and episcopal leadership in the 1980s has overshadowed the substantive changes in American Catholicism that have taken place in the parish. Beginning slowly in the years after Vatican II, the changes in parish and religious life have continued in the 1980s. No aspect of parish or religious life has escaped this change.

Certainly the most visible change in the past few years has been the shift in parish leadership from the clergy to the laity. To be sure, the priest is still the single most important source of authority in any parish. Parishes in the 1980s have not become democracies, but neither are they the autocracies of the 1950s. Parish councils have provided forums for the discussion of parish issues and many pastors have welcomed this opportunity to share their decision making. The result has been a collaborative leadership style unknown before Vatican II; finances, religious education, youth work, liturgy—all have been shaped by the decisions of parish councils.

The area where this collaborative leadership has had the most notable impact has been the liturgy. Many parish councils have established subcommittees to develop new liturgies for the parish, and the end result has been services that reflect the interests and heritage of the parish. Most important is that the laity has a greater role in all of these liturgies.

The increased involvement of the laity in parish affairs has meant an expanded role for women in the Church. ''When a

Catholic woman stood at the altar in 1960,'' noted Mary O'Connell in the June 1987 issue of *U.S. Catholic,* ''it meant only one thing: she was getting married. In 1987, she may be reading Scripture, distributing communion, or leading a prayer service.'' Yet this expanded role has reminded many Catholic women that there are limits to their work within the Church. By virtue of their sex, they are forever prohibited from ordination to the priesthood. The anger and frustration of many Catholic women has become a topic of concern and discussion among the American Catholic bishops and will be the subject of their next major pastoral letter. Yet, without significant moves toward the ordination of women—extremely unlikely, given the unqualified opposition of the Vatican—this issue will be part of American Catholicism well into the next century.

As the role of the laity in parish life has been expanding in the 1980s, the roles of priests and nuns have been diminishing. The years after Vatican II witnessed an exodus of priests and nuns from the religious life, a departure that was exacerbated by a simultaneous decline in the number of people entering vocations. The end result has been a substantially diminished presence of professed religious within the parish. Indeed, there are many parishes where the pastor has no religious colleagues at all and others where there is no full-time pastor.

This shortage has forced dioceses and bishops to become more imaginative in how priests are utilized. Some dioceses have begun to assign teams of priests to serve a region rather than a single parish. Other dioceses have shifted priests out of administrative positions into parish work. Still other dioceses have begun to recruit religious orders to take responsibility for selected parishes. In every diocese, however, bishops and pastors have become increasingly dependent on the growing corps of lay deacons who perform many of the duties—baptisms and sick visitations, for example—that were once the exclusive domain of the priesthood.

The shrinking number of priests has been matched by the declining number of women religious and the real impact has been felt in the parish. Because there were fewer sisters, there were fewer teachers available for parochial schools. Without the aid of nuns to staff their classrooms, pastors have been forced to hire more lay teachers. Rising costs and an inability to hire qualified teachers has been a major cause of school closings around the country. By the mid-1980s, enrollment in American Catholic parochial schools was less than half of the peak reached in the mid-1960s.

There is an ironic twist to this decline. As the number of Catholic schools has diminished, student testing has revealed that students do better academically in parochial schools than in public schools. "Catholic students gained the equivalent of one grade level more [than public school pupils]," noted one university researcher. Even more startling is the recent data showing how well black and Hispanic students do in parochial schools. Although the results are preliminary, a recent University of Michigan study gives some indication that minorities in Catholic schools take more academic courses, score higher on reading tests, and go to college in greater numbers than their public school counterparts.

There is no question that parochial education will continue into the next century, but the days of the school as a standard parish institution are gone. A more likely prospect is several parishes pooling resources to support a single regional parochial school. It also can be hoped that suburban Catholics will assume some responsibility for assisting inner-city parish schools—important institutions for Catholic minorities.

CONCLUSION. In a 1987 pastoral letter marking the bicentennial of the U.S. Constitution, Archbishop Francis Stafford of Denver called on his fellow Catholics to recommit themselves to the moral and political traditions of two centuries past. He further agreed that the decline in mainline Protestantism and the divisiveness of evangelistic denominations has created an opportunity for "a Catholic movement in the ongoing and never-to-be completed evolution of the American experiment."

Archbishop Stafford's optimism about the Church as it approaches a new century is a far cry from knowing the future contours of American Catholicism. Undoubtedly the American Church of the twenty-first century will be different, but how and in what ways? Recent demographic and sociological studies do offer some indications of the future of the Church in this country.

It is likely that the Church will become increasingly dependent on lay people to provide the support services once provided by priests and nuns. Lay deacons will do more preaching, baptizing, sick visitation, and provide more of the pastoral care. Nuns will virtually disappear from the parochial classroom, replaced in the select number of parishes willing to support a school by a corps of committed lay teachers.

The increasing involvement of the laity in parish affairs will necessarily make the American Church more democratic. Councils dominated by the laity will assume additional responsibilities for the day-to-day temporal operations of the parish. So also, the laity will become increasingly involved in planning parish liturgies and other theological issues.

Greater lay involvement will mean that the leadership of the Church at all levels will become even more collegial and collaborative than at present. Pastors will consult with their parishioners and bishops will consult with their pastors and religious before diocesan policy is established. In this same manner, the collegial tradition of American Catholicism will be enhanced the bishops regularly addressing the important issues facing both Church and nation.

One of the more subtle but substantive changes that will take place in American Catholicism during the first half of the next century is the return of ethnicity within the Church. Demographers are predicting that by the year 2050, a majority of American Catholics will be of Hispanic origin. So also, the number of black Catholics will increase substantially. By the middle of the next century, therefore, it is likely that American Catholicism will once again be a mosaic of several different cultural traditions.

Above all, recent scholarship reveals that American Catholicism is becoming a people's church, increasingly "American" in its content and form, and more and more like other Christian denominations in this country. There is little doubt that this American style will continue to perplex and confuse the Vatican and precipitate continued misunderstandings over a variety of religious and social issues. Yet the process of Americanization will not be stopped or reversed by Vatican fiat. For more than four centuries, since the establishment of the first Catholic parish in 1565, Catholics have influenced and have been influenced by American society. Sustaining this special relationship without alienating Rome will be the challenge of American Catholicism in the next century.

Part II

READINGS

READING NO. 1

BISHOP CALDERON ON THE FLORIDA MISSIONS, 1674*

In the seventeenth and eighteenth centuries, the Spanish established a series of missions along the southern and western rims of what is now the United States. These missions served as bases for efforts to convert the Indians to Christianity and to explore the continent. The success of the mission system varied from region to region. In Florida, Texas, and New Mexico, the missions struggled to survive; in Arizona and California, the missions were a qualified success. In no region did the missions succeed in their goal of dominating and converting a majority of the Indians. In the passage that follows, a local bishop reports on the impoverished state of the Florida missions more than a century after they were established.

γ   γ   γ

. . . What has been discovered, up to today, concerning the entire district of Florida, both along the seacoast and inland, is as follows:

On the coast of the northern border, 30 leagues from Cape Canaveral, [where] the canal of Bahama disembogues, is located, on the 30th parallel of latitude, the city of Saint Augustine which was founded about 1559 [1565] by the Adelantado Pedro Menéndes Aviles. It is the capital of the provinces of Florida and has more than 300 Spanish inhabitants, soldiers and married people. Its harbor is very secure by reason of a very dangerous sand bar which it has at its entrance, which shifts its position in storms and at high tide has 20 spans of

---

*Quoted from Lucy L. Wenhold, ed., "A Seventeenth Century Letter of Gabriel Diaz Vara Calderon, Bishop of Cuba Describing the Indians and Indian Missions of Florida," *Smithsonian Miscellaneous Collections,* 95 (1936): 7-9, 14.

water. The city is built lengthwise from north to south. It is almost cut off by an arm of the sea which surrounds it and buffets it, leaving it half submerged from hurricanes as it lies at sea level. Its climate is somewhat unhealthful, being very cold in winter, with freezes, and excessively hot in summer, both of which extremes are felt the more as there is no protection nor defence in the houses, they being of wood with board walls. The soil is sand and therefore unproductive; no wheat grows, and corn only sparsely and at the cost of much labor. Thus the inhabitants are compelled regularly to depend for their sustenance upon the products of the province of Apalache. The section does not produce any sort of raw material which could attract trade, and has no resources other than the government allowance, which it awaits each year from the city of Mexico, and by which the infantry is fed and clothed.

As regards its spiritual welfare, it has a parish church dedicated to Saint Augustine, served by a priest, a sacristan and acolytes, and a Franciscan convent, headquarters for the province, called Saint Helena, with three monks [*sic*], a superior, a preacher, a lay brother, and with authority by a royal decree of Your Majesty to have three curates for the three principal languages of these provinces, Guale, Timuqua and Apalache, for the teaching of Christian doctrine and the administering of the sacraments to the Indians who usually attend to the cultivating of the lands of the residents of the Post [Saint Augustine]. Of the four hermitages which formerly existed, only two remain: San Patricio and Our Lady of Solitude, and a hospital contiguous to the latter with six beds. For defense there is a fortress with 20 guns and a good garrison, a governor resident in the city, a sergeant-major, 2 captains, 300 enlisted men, and 2 royal officials.

Going out of the city, at half a league to the north there is a small village of scarcely more than 30 Indian inhabitants, called Nombre de Dios, the mission which is served by the convent. Following the road from east to west, within an extent of 98 leagues there are 24 settlements and missions of Christian Indians, 11 belonging to the province of Timuqua and 13 to that of Apalache. . . .

As to their religion, they are not idolators, and they embrace with devotion the mysteries of our holy faith. They attend mass with regularity at 11 o'clock on the holy days they observe, namely, Sunday, and the festivals of Christmas, the Circumcision, Epiphany, the Purification of Our Lady, and the days of Saint Peter, Saint Paul and All Saints Day, and before entering the church each one brings to the house of the priest as a contribution a log of wood. They do not talk in the church, and the women are separated from the men; the former on the side of the Epistle, the latter on the side of the Evangel [Gospel]. They are very devoted to the Virgin, and on Saturdays they attend when her mass is sung. On Sundays they attend the *Rosario* and the *Salve* in the afternoon. They celebrate with rejoicing and devotion to the Birth of Our Lord, all attending the midnight mass with offerings of loaves, eggs and other food. They subject themselves to extraordinary penances during Holy Week, and during the 24 hours of Holy Thursday and Friday, while our Lord is in the Urn of the Monument, they attend standing, praying the rosary in complete silence, 24 men and 24 women and the same number of children of both sexes, with hourly changes. The children, both male and female, go to the church on work days, to a religious school where they are taught by a teacher whom they call *Athequi* of the church; [a person] whom the priests have for this service; as they have also a person deputized to report to them concerning all parishioners who live in evil.

READING NO. 2

THE DEATH OF ISAAC JOGUES AMONG THE IROQUOIS, 1647*

The personal heroism and sacrifice of the French missionary priests in the New World were extraordinary by every standard. Often caught in the midst of Indian tribes at war, many of these priests sacrificed their lives for the cause of Christianity. Accounts of the exploits of one missionary order, the Society of Jesus also known as the Jesuits, were published and distributed throughout France. The Relations, *as they were titled, provide the basic documentation for the contemporary study of the French missionary experience in the New World. In the passage below from* The Relations, *Father Gabriel Lalemant describes the torture and death of one of the great French missionary priests, Isaac Jogues.*

γ   γ   γ

. . . Hardly had the poor Father been refreshed among us two or three months, when he recommenced his expeditions; on the twenty-fourth of September in the same year, 1646, he embarks with a young Frenchman, in a canoe conducted by some Hurons, in order to return to the land of his crosses. He had strong premonitions of his death. . . . We have learned that he was slain directly upon his entrance into that country full of murder and blood: here follows a letter announcing this, from the Governor of the Dutch to Monsieur the Chevalier de Mont-Magny. . . .

"For the rest, I have not much to tell you, except how the French arrived, on the 17th of this present month of October, 1647, at the fort of the Maquois. . . . The very day of their coming, they began to threaten them,—and that immediately, with heavy blows of fists and clubs, saying: 'You will die tomorrow: be not astonished. But we will not burn you; have

*Quoted from Reuben G. Thwaites, ed., *The Jesuit Relations and Allied Documents* (Cleveland, 1898), vol. 31, pp. 118–119.

courage; we will strike you with the hatchet and will set your heads on the palings,' (that is to say, on the fence above their village) 'so that when we shall capture your brothers they may still see you.' You must know that it was only the nation of the bear which put them to death; the nations of the wolf and the turtle did all that they could to save their lives, and said to the nation of the bear: 'Kill us first.' But, alas! they are not in life for all that. Know, then, that on the 18th, in the evening, when they came to call Isaac to supper, he got up and went away with that Barbarian to the lodge of the bear. There was a traitor with his hatchet behind the door, who, on entering, split open his head; then immediately he cut it off, and set it on the palings. The next day, very early, he did the same to the other man, and their bodies were thrown into the river. Monsieur, I have not been able to know or to learn from any Savage why they have killed them. . . .''

Such is, word for word, what the Dutch have written concerning the death of Father Isaac Jogues. . . .

READING NO. 3

EUSEBIO KINO ON THE ARIZONA MISSIONS, 1710*

The Arizona missions were a qualified success for the Spanish missionaries. This achievement was due in large part to one man—the Italian Jesuit, Eusebio Kino. This legendary missionary arrived in Arizona in 1687 to work among the Pima Indians. Kino succeeded where others had failed because he accepted the Indians on their own terms, quietly introducing a number of improvements in the quality of Pima life. The Pima, in turn, accepted Kino and his Catholicism precisely because he had helped the tribe without any expectation of reciprocation. In the passage below, Kino reports to his superiors on the vast new territory he had explored over the previous two decades.

γ   γ   γ

With all these expeditions or missions which have been made to a distance of two hundred leagues in these new heathendoms in these twenty-one years, there have been brought to our friendship and to the desire of receiving our holy Catholic faith, between Pimas, Cocomaricopas, Yumas, Quiquimas, etc., more than thirty thousand souls, there being sixteen thousand of Pimas alone. I have solemnized more than four thousand baptisms, and I could have baptized ten or twelve thousand Indians more if the lack of father laborers had not rendered it impossible for us to catechise them and instruct them in advance. But if our Lord sends, by means of his royal Majesty and of the superiors, the necessary fathers for so great and so ripe a harvest of souls, it will not be difficult, God willing, to achieve the holy baptism of all these souls and of very many others, on the very populous Colorado River, as well as in California Alta, and at thirty-five degrees latitude

*Quoted from Herbert E. Bolton, ed., *Kino's Historical Memoir of Pimeria Alta.* (Cleveland, 1919), vol. 2, pp. 252–253.

and thereabouts, for this very great Colorado River has its origin at fifty-two degrees latitude.

And here I answer the question asked of me in the letter of the Father Rector Juan Hurtasum, as to whether some rivers run into the North Sea or all empty into the Sea of California, by saying that as this Colorado River, which is the Rio del Norte of the ancients, carries so much water, it must be that it comes from a high and remote land, as is the case with the other large volumed rivers of all the world and terraqueous globe; therefore the other rivers of the land of fifty-two degrees latitude probably have their slope toward the Sea of the North, where Husson wintered. Some more information can be drawn from the maps which I add to this report; and in order not to violate the brevity which I promised herein, I will add only that in regard to the fourteen journeys for two hundred leagues to the northwest, I have written a little treatise of about twenty-five sheets which is entitled "Cosmographical Proof that California is not an Island but a Peninsula," etc.; and that of these new discoveries and new conversions in general, by order of our Father-General, Thirso Gonzales. I am writing another and more extensive treatise with maps, of which more than one hundred sheets are already written. By suggestion of his Reverence it is entitled "Celestial Favors of Jesus Our Lord, and of Mary Most Holy, and of the Most Glorious Apostle of the Indies, San Francisco Xavier, experienced in the New Conversions of these New Nations of these New Heathendoms of this North America."

READING NO. 4

JUNIPERO SERRA ON THE CALIFORNIA MISSIONS, 1784*

The success of the California missions was largely depen-dent on the Franciscan priest, Junipero Serra. Serra's great-est skills were in administration and during his fifteen years in California from 1769 to 1784, he founded nine missions along the coast from San Diego to San Francisco. Serra was aided in his achievement by a number of other factors. He was able to gather committed priests to staff his mission churches. The California climate was conducive to raising cattle, growing fruit, and cultivating grapes for wine. Finally, the Indians of California were less hostile than Indians in other regions of the country. In the passage below, Serra describes the agri-cultural and spiritual bounty of one of his final years in Cal-ifornia.

γ   γ   γ

. . . We can consider this the happiest year of the mission [1783] because the number of baptisms was one hundred seventy-five and of marriages thirty-six.

The sowing of all grains amounted to eighty-four bushels, eight pecks. This included one bushel and a half of wheat, half a bushel of corn, and two pecks of beans, which were sown for the [Lower] California Indians, who had moved here and were married in this mission.

And the harvest, less the amount of forty-seven bushels which belonged to these Indians and other concessions made to the people such as a portion of the barley which they might reap and some twenty bushels of wheat from the chaff of the threshing, which was stored in the mission granaries amounted to twenty-six hundred fourteen and a half bushels, that is, of measured barley six hundred seventy bushels, eight

*Quoted from John Tracy Ellis, ed., *Documents of American Catholic History* (Milwaukee, 1956), pp. 44–45.

hundred thirty-five of wheat, only two hundred according to our estimate are kept in the ear. There were nine hundred seventy-one bushels of corn of both kinds according to our estimate, sixty-three bushels of peas, sixteen bushels of horse beans, four bushels of lentils, and fifty-three bushels of various kinds of beans.

Today the new Christians of this mission number six hundred fourteen living persons, even though some of them take a leave of absence from time to time. They have been maintained and are maintained without any scarcity and we supplied the quartermaster of the presidio of San Carlos with one hundred thirty bushels of Indian corn; because they did not ask for more, also with thirty bushels of beans. The escort of this mission, at the request of the ensign quartermaster, received rations in these two kinds of grain. There have not been other deliveries of consequence so that in our prudent judgment of the two chief commodities, wheat and corn, about half the amount harvested may still remain.

The value of the food supplied to the presidio has been paid already in cloth, which now covers the Indians who grew the crops, but at that we are still distressed at the sight of so much nudity among them.

We do not get clothing now from the soldiers, as we did formerly, not even from those who have debts to us no matter how small. The wool, which in some of the missions is enough to cover Indian nakedness, here has not been any help to us so far, because the thefts of sheep are so numerous that already for more than three years, we can not exceed two hundred head between goats and sheep, and from shearing the few that we have we get nothing worthwhile.

The condition, then, of the Mission in things spiritual is that up to this day in this Mission:

Baptisms. 1,006
Confirmations 936
    And since those of the other missions
    belong in some way to this it is noted
    in passing that their number is 5,307
Marriages in this mission. 259
Burials 356

The number of Christian families living at the mission and eating jointly, as well as widowers, single men, and children of both sexes, is evident from the enclosed census lists and so is omitted here.

They pray twice daily with the priest in the church. More than one hundred twenty of them confess in Spanish and many who have died used to do it as well. The others confess as best they can. They work at all kinds of mission labor, such as farm hands, herdsmen, cowboys, shepherds, milkers, diggers, gardeners, carpenters, farmers, irrigators, reapers, blacksmiths, sacristans, and they do everything else that comes along for their corporal and spiritual welfare. . . .

READING NO. 5

CATHOLICISM IN MARYLAND IN 1638*

The majority of British Catholics who were brave enough to risk their lives on a perilous ocean voyage chose the colony of Maryland as their destination. A handful of English Jesuits were among the first settlers of the colony and it was the Jesuits who nurtured and sustained the Maryland Catholic community for the next 150 years. To support themselves, these priests established farms and became planters and traders as well as missionaries. It was the Jesuits, traveling to all parts of the colony, who gave visibility to Maryland Catholicism in the colonial era. In the passage below, an anonymous Jesuit reports to his superiors on early missionary activities in the colony.

γ   γ   γ

Four Fathers gave their attention to this Mission, with one assistant in temporal affairs; and he, indeed, after enduring severe toils for the space of five years, with the greatest patience, humility, and ardent love, chanced to be seized by the disease prevailing at the time, and happily exchanged this wretched life for an immortal one.

He was also shortly followed by one of the Fathers, who was young indeed, but on account of his remarkable qualities of mind, evidently of great promise. He had scarcely spent two months in this mission, when, to the great grief of all of us, he was carried off by the common sickness prevailing in the Colony, from which no one of the three remaining priests has escaped unharmed; yet we have not ceased to labor, to the best of our ability among the neighboring people.

And though the rulers of the Colony have not yet allowed us to dwell among the savages, both on account of the prevailing sickness, and also, because of the hostile disposition which

---

*Quoted from E.A. Dalrymple, ed., *Narrative of a Voyage to Maryland by Father Andrew White, S.J.* (Baltimore, 1874), pp. 54-62.

the barbarians evince towards the English, they having slain a man from this Colony, who was staying among them for the sake of trading, and having also entered into a conspiracy against our whole nation; yet we hope that one of us will shortly secure a station among the barbarians. Meanwhile, we devote ourselves more zealously to the English; and since there are Protestants as well as Catholics in the Colony, we have labored for both, and God has blessed our labors.

For, among the Protestants, nearly all who have come from England, in this year 1638, and many others, have been converted to the faith, together with four servants, whom we purchased in Virginia, (another Colony of our Kingdom), for necessary services, and five mechanics, whom we hired for a month, and have in the meantime won to God. Not long afterwards, one of these, after being duly prepared for death, by receiving the sacraments, departed this life. And among these persons hardly anything else worth mentioning has occurred. . . .

Besides these, one of us, going out of the Colony, found two Frenchmen, one of whom had been without the sacraments of the Catholic Church for three entire years; the other, who was already near death, having spent fifteen whole years among Heretics, had lived just as they do. The Father aided the former with the sacraments and confirmed him in the Catholic faith as much as he could. The latter he restored to the Catholic Church, and, administering all the sacraments, prepared him for dying happily.

As for the Catholics, the attendance on the sacraments here is so large, that it is not greater among the Europeans, in proportion to the number of Catholics. The more ignorant have been catechised, and Catechetical Lectures have been delivered for the more advanced every Sunday; but, on Feast days sermons have been rarely neglected. The sick and the dying, who have been very numerous this year, and who dwelt far apart, we have assisted in every way, so that not even a single one has died without the sacraments. We have buried very many, and baptized various persons. And, although there are not wanting frequent occasions of dissension, yet none of any importance has arisen here in the last nine months, which we have not immediately allayed. By the blessing of God, we have this consolation, that no vices spring up among the new Catholics, although settlements of this kind are not usually supplied from the best class of men.

We bought off in Virginia, two Catholics, who had sold themselves into bondage, nor was the money ill-spent, for both showed themselves good Christians: one, indeed, surpasses the ordinary standard. Some others have performed the same duty of Charity, buying thence Catholic servants, who are very numerous in that country. For every year, very many sell themselves thither into bondage, and living among men of the worst example, and, being destitute of all spiritual aid, they generally make shipwreck of their souls.

In the case of one, we adore the remarkable providence and mercy of God, which brought a man encompassed in the world with very many difficulties, and now at length living in Virginia, almost continually without any aid to his soul, to undertake these exercises, not long before his death. This design a severe sickness prevented, which he bore with the greatest patience, with a mind generally fixed on God; and at length having properly received all the sacraments in the most peaceful manner, beyond what is usual, renders back to the Creator the breath of the life that remained, which had been so full of troubles and disquietudes. . . .

READING NO. 6

THE PERSECUTION OF MARYLAND CATHOLICS IN 1656*

When they arrived in Maryland in 1634, Catholics were on equal terms with Protestants, a situation that was unique in the British colonies. Over the next fifteen years this denominational equality was codified by the Maryland assembly and culminated in the "Act Concerning Religion" in 1649. But religious freedom did not last much beyond the passage of the Act. In 1654, a Puritan-dominated assembly repealed the Act and let loose an anti-Catholic tirade. Farms owned by the Society of Jesus were plundered and priests and laity were forced to flee or go into hiding. In the passage below, an anonymous Jesuit describes the attacks on Catholicism during one of the worst years in Maryland history.

γ   γ   γ

In Maryland, during the year last past [1655], our people have escaped grievous dangers, and have had to contend with great difficulties and straits, and have suffered many unpleasant things as well from enemies as from our own people. The English who inhabit Virginia had made an attack on the colonists, themselves Englishmen too; and safety being guaranteed on certain conditions, received indeed the governor of Maryland, with many others in surrender; but the conditions being treacherously violated, four of the captives, and three of them catholics, were pierced with leaden balls. Rushing into our houses, they demanded for death the impostors, as they called them, intending inevitable slaughter to those who should be caught. But the fathers, by the protection of God, unknown to them, were carried from before their faces: their books, furniture, and whatever was in the house, fell a prey to the robbers. With almost the entire loss of their property, private and do-

*Quoted from E.A. Dalrymple, ed., *Narrative of a Voyage to Maryland of Father Andrew White, S.J.* (Baltimore, 1874), pp. 91–93.

mestic, together with great peril of life, they were secretly carried into Virginia; and in the greatest want of necessaries, scarcely, and with difficulty, do they sustain life. They live in a mean hut, low and depressed, not much unlike a cistern, or even a tomb, in which that great defender of the faith, St. Athanasius, lay concealed for many years. To their other miseries this inconvenience was added, that whatever comfort or aid this year, under name of stipend, from pious men in England, was destined for them, had been lost, the ship being intercepted in which it was carried. But nothing affects them more than that there is not a supply of wine, which is sufficient to perform the sacred mysteries of the altar. They have no servant, either for domestic use, or for directing their way through unknown and suspected places, or even to row and steer the boat, if at any time there is need. Often, over spacious and vast rivers, one of them, alone and unaccompanied, passes and repasses long distances, with no other pilot directing his course than Divine Providence. By and by the enemy may be gone and they may return to Maryland: the things which they have already suffered from their people, and the disadvantages which still threaten are not much more tolerable.

READING NO. 7

CHARLES CARROLL ON RELIGIOUS TOLERATION, 1773*

Catholicism was a suspect religion for most of the colonial era in British America. By 1692, Catholics were obliged to pay taxes for the support of the Anglican Church and in later years they were denied the vote, prohibited from practicing their religion in public, and forbidden to establish schools for the instruction of their children. Perhaps it was because of these indignities that colonial Catholics were among the most ardent supporters of religious toleration and political independence. In the passage that follows, Charles Carroll of Carrollton, a leading Maryland Catholic and later a signer of the Declaration of Independence, attacks the religious prejudice of a political foe and defends the right of Catholics to practice their faith.

γ   γ   γ

. . . The Citizen did not deliver his sentiment only but likewise the sentiment of others. We Catholics, who think we were hardly treated on occasion, *we* still remember the treatment though our resentment hath entirely subsided. It is not in the least surprizing that a man incapable of forming an exalted sentiment, should not readily comprehend the force and beauty of one. . . . To what purpose was the threat thrown out of enforcing the penal statutes by proclamation? Why am I told that my conduct is very inconsistent with the situation of one, who "owes even the *toleration* he enjoys to the favour of government"? If by instilling prejudices into the Governor, and by every mean and wicked artifice you can rouse the popular resentment against certain religionists, and thus bring on a persecution of them, it will then be known whether the toleration I enjoy, be due to the favour of government or not. . . .

*Quoted from Kate Mason Rowland, *The Life of Charles Carroll of Carrollton, 1737–1832*. (New York, 1898), vol. 1, p. 359.

READING NO. 8

JOHN CARROLL ON AMERICAN CATHOLICISM IN 1785*

With the end of the Revolutionary War in 1783, the challenge facing Catholics was to build a national church. Now that they were free to practice their faith as they saw fit, what sort of denomination would Catholics establish? Who would lead the Church in the United States? What sort of schools, hospitals, asylums, convents, and seminaries would be needed? The Vatican left these matters in the hands of another member of the Carroll family. In 1784, Father John Carroll, cousin of Charles, was named by the Vatican to be the superior of the American Catholic missions. In the reading below, Carroll reports to Rome on the state of American Catholicism in 1785.

γ γ γ

. . . In Maryland a few of the leading more wealthy families still profess the Catholic faith introduced at the very foundation of the province by their ancestors. The greater part of them are planters and in Pennsylvania almost all are farmers, except the merchants and mechanics living in Philadelphia. As for piety, they are for the most part sufficiently assiduous in the exercises of religion and in frequenting the sacraments, but they lack that fervor, which frequent appeals to the sentiment of piety usually produce, as many congregations hear the word of God only once a month, and sometimes only once in two months. We are reduced to this by want of priests, by the distance of congregations from each other and by difficulty of travelling. This refers to Catholics born here, for the condition of the Catholics who in great numbers are flowing in here from different countries of Europe, is very different. For while there are few of our native Catholics who do not approach the

---

*Quoted from John G. Shea, *History of the Catholic Church in the United States* (New York, 1888), vol. 2, pp. 258–259.

sacraments of Penance and the Holy Eucharist, at least once a year, especially in Easter time, you can scarcely find any among the newcomers who discharge this duty of religion, and there is reason to fear that the example will be very pernicious especially in commercial towns. The abuses that have grown among Catholics are chiefly those, which result with unavoidable intercourse with non-Catholics, and the examples thense derived: namely more free intercourse between young people of opposite sexes than is compatible with chastity in mind and body; too great fondness for dances and similar amusements; and an incredible eagerness, especially in girls, for reading love stories which are brought over in great quantities from Europe. Then among other things, a general lack of care in instructing their children and especially the negro slaves in their religion, as these people are kept constantly at work, so that they rarely hear any instructions from the priest, unless they can spend a short time with one; and most of them are consequently very dull in faith and depraved in morals. It can scarcely be believed how much trouble and care they give the pastors of souls. . . .

READING NO. 9

JOHN CARROLL IS APPOINTED FIRST U.S. CATHOLIC BISHOP, 1789*

Two important events took place in 1789 that would profoundly affect the course of American Catholicism for the next two centuries. In April, a new federal government was established under the recently ratified Constitution. It was a government with checks and balances that would soon codify religious liberty in a Bill of Rights. Another, less noticed event took place in November when the Vatican appointed John Carroll to be the first Catholic bishop in the United States. It was the Vatican's recognition that Catholicism was no longer a persecuted denomination in the United States. In the reading below, the Vatican formally announces Carroll's appointment as bishop.

γ   γ   γ

. . . Now all things being materially weighed and considered in this Congregation, it was easily agreed that the interests and increase of Catholic religion would be greatly promoted if an episcopal see were erected at Baltimore, and the said John Carroll were appointed the Bishop of it. We, therefore, to whom this opinion has been reported by our beloved son, Cardinal Antonelli, Prefect of the said Congregation, having nothing more at heart than to ensure success to whatever tends to the propagation of true religion, and to the honor and increase of the Catholic Church, by the plenitude of our apostolical power, and by the tenor of these presents, do establish and erect the aforesaid town of Baltimore into an episcopal see forever, for one Bishop to be chosen by us in all future vacancies; and We, therefore, by the apostolical authority aforesaid, do allow, grant and permit to the Bishop of the said city and to his successors in all future times, to exercise

*Quoted from John G. Shea, *History of the Catholic Church in the United States* (New York, 1888), vol. 2, pp. 340–342

episcopal power and jurisdiction, and every other episcopal function which Bishops constituted in other places are empowered to hold and enjoy in their respective churches, cities and dioceses, by right, custom, or by other means, by general privileges, graces, indults and apostolical dispensations, together with all pre-eminences, honors, immunities, graces and favors, which other Cathedral Churches, by right or custom, or any other sort, have, hold and enjoy. We moreover decree and declare the said Episcopal see thus erected to be subject or suffragan to no Metropolitan right or jurisdiction, but to be forever subject, immediately to us and to our successors the Roman Pontiffs, and to this Apostolical See. And till another opportunity shall be presented to us of establishing other Catholic Bishops in the United States of America, and till other dispositions shall be made by this apostolical See. We declare, by our apostolical authority, all the faithful of Christ, living in Catholic communion, as well ecclesiastics as seculars, and all the clergy and people dwelling of the aforesaid United States of America, though hitherto they may have been subject to other Bishops of other dioceses, to be henceforward subject to the Bishop of Baltimore in all future times; And whereas by special grant, and for this first time only, we have allowed the priests exercising the care of souls in the United States of America, to elect a person to be appointed Bishop by us, and almost all their votes have been given to our beloved Son, John Carroll, Priest; We being otherwise certified of his faith, prudence, piety, and zeal, forasmuch as by our mandate he hath during the late years directed the spiritual government of souls, do therefore by the plenitude of our authority, declare, create, appoint and constitute the said John Carroll, Bishop and Pastor of the said Church of Baltimore, granting to him the faculty of receiving the rite of consecration from any Catholic bishop holding communion with the apostolical see, assisted by two ecclesiastics, vested with some dignity, in case that two bishops cannot be had, first having taken the usual oath according to the Roman Pontifical. . . .

READING NO. 10

NEW YORK CATHOLICS PETITION FOR PROTESTANT AID, 1810*

Throughout John Carroll's tenure as bishop and later arch-bishop of Baltimore (1789–1815), American Catholicism was administered almost entirely on the parish level. Each individual parish was left to raise the funds needed to build and operate its churches and schools. To be sure, Carroll and his fellow bishops reserved the right to appoint the pastors of these parishes, but temporal affairs remained firmly in the hands of lay trustees during these years.

The job of parish trustee was not an easy one. The small number of communicants and the general poverty of the Catholic population made it difficult to raise operating funds. In the reading below, the trustees of one parish in New York petition their Protestant neighbors for financial assistance.

γ   γ   γ

The Trustees of St. Peter's Church in the City of New York beg leave most respectfully to state to the Rector, Church Wardens and Vestry of Trinity Church.

That, Since the adoption of that liberal and happy constitution under which they live, and which grants to all, an equal participation in all the rights and privileges of Citizens, together with the free exercise of their religious Sentiments agreeably to the dictates of their respective consciences, having in common with every other Society and Denomination of Christians considerably increased in number and far beyond the contracted walls of their present Church will admit they were compelled to undertake for the accommodation of a very large portion of their members to erect a new Church upon a plan which should in some degree comport with the honor and majesty of that Deity in whom all Christians confide, as well as answer at the same time the above-mentioned object.

*Quoted from *American Catholic Historical Researches,* 29 (1912):223–224.

That after repeatedly exerting all their endeavors and straining every nerve to collect from the different members of their own Congregation, the sums necessary for the completion of this pious undertaking, they observe with the deepest concern that they have fallen far short in consequence of their poverty of what they thought they had reason to expect and calculate upon from their number.

That having now no other resource left (their small funds being entirely exhausted in what has been already done towards the erection of said Church) but in the benevolence of their respectable Fellow Citizens of other Denominations, confident of your generosity from the pleasing remembrance of former favours conferred on them by the worthy members composing your Corporation, acquainted with your resources and relying upon your Charity which has been so frequently and so conspicuously exerted in behalf of others under somewhat similar circumstances, they take the liberty once more to solicit in a particular manner your kind aid and humbly request a further extension of your benevolence.

They flatter themselves and feel the strongest assurance, that whilst engaged in one common cause, to wit: the promotion of the happiness of our fellow Citizens by diffusing among them a spirit of piety, religion and morality, your zeal for the good of mankind will not permit you to withhold that assistance from them, which will tend so greatly to encourage and enable them to carry into extensive effect their benevolent intentions.

They beg leave also to assure you that they feel the greatest happiness in experiencing that the former expression of your liberality and good will towards St. Peter's Church, for which the Trustees offer their sincere acknowledgments, has contributed not a little to promote that harmony and concord which at present subsist between them and the Congregation with which you are united, and which it will be ever their earnest wish and desire to cherish and maintain.

READING NO. 11

AMBROSE MARECHAL ON AMERICAN CATHOLICISM IN 1818*

The task of leading the American Catholic Church was not easy and the burden is most evident in the periodic reports sent to Rome by the archbishops of Baltimore. John Carroll was well aware of the enormity of the responsibility when he accepted his episcopal appointment in 1789. He knew that to organize a church he would need a devout and loyal clergy and an enlightened laity. Yet try as he might, Carroll was never able to find enough priests or win the undivided loyalty of the laity. Carroll's successor, Ambrose Marechal, inherited these problems. In the reading below, Marechal reports to Rome on the chronic shortage of priests and nuns and the periodic rebellions of the laity. Marechal seemed hopeless to resolve these problems.

γ   γ   γ

. . . There is no region in the world, where the Catholic religion can be propagated more quickly or widely and where it exists more securely than in the United States of America. Here there is no danger whatsoever that converts to the faith will suffer persecution or that their churches will be destroyed by the arbitrary command of some tyrant, as often occurs in the Chinese Empire and in the other missions of the Indes. All religions, which recognize Christ as the Saviour of the world, are tolerated here, and the laws of the Republic protect them all and most severely punish those who attempt to disturb the divine worship of any sect. And since religious liberty is the fundamental principle of the American Republic, there is no magistrate from the President to the least official, who can with impunity molest Catholics even in the slightest way. The only danger that blocks the path of our most holy religion,

*Quoted from John Tracy Ellis, ed., *Documents of American Catholic History* (Milwaukee, 1956), pp. 218–220.

consists in the internal dissensions which divide the faithful against each other. The magistrates do not care about these dissensions. Only offenses which affect public peace and the liberty of the citizens are punished by the civil law. The nations which border our republic profess the Catholic religion. These are Canada, Florida and Mexico. Besides there is a very large number of Catholics in our United States. The Protestants, who constitute the greatest part of the citizens, have almost completely rejected the prejudices under which they formerly labored, and they look upon the Catholic religion with a certain amount of veneration. There is also an immense number of Europeans, who come hither daily, and among them there are many Catholics. It seems that this immigration will not be lessened for a number of years. Since the American republic possesses such an extensive territory, it might easily sustain, by the millions, those who migrate to it, and it is evident that the multitudes, who come to America from Europe, will not be quickly diminished. If the Sacred Congregation ponders over these facts it will perceive clearly that there is no region which offers a wider or more fertile field for apostolic zeal.

However we do have many difficulties here that must be overcome:

Insufficient number of missionaries. Young American ladies, who formerly could scarcely refrain from laughing aloud when they heard Europeans telling of nuns living uninterruptedly in monasteries, now embrace the religious life so willingly, that I must needs exercise vigilance lest more than can be cared for be admitted to the monasteries which exist in my diocese. But it is an altogether different story with regard to youths embracing the clerical state. Some are deterred by celibacy; others are frightened away by the labors of acquiring a knowledge of the ecclesiastical sciences, for this takes a long time and must be undertaken before ordination; but most of all they are afraid of the poverty which is suffered by missionaries, who exercise the sacred ministry in the country districts. For with a little industry on their part, they can hope to live in comfort, nay even in abundance, if they engage in commerce or agriculture. . . .

The schisms which occur very frequently in these regions. It is of the greatest concern that the Sacred Congregation know accurately their principal cause. It should therefore be noted:—1. that the American people pursue with a most ardent love the civil liberty which they enjoy. For the principle of civil liberty is paramount with them, so that absolutely all the magistrates, from the highest to the lowest, are elected by popular vote at determined times in the year. Likewise all the Protestant sects, who constitute the greater part of the people, are governed by these same principles, and as a result they elect and dismiss their pastors at will. Catholics in turn, living in their midst, are evidently exposed to the danger of admitting the same principles of ecclesiastical government. Clever and impious priests, who flatter them and appeal to their pride, easily lead them to believe that they also possess the right of choosing their pastors and dismissing them as they please. 2. When the Catholics in some part of my diocese become numerous enough to think that they can build a church, first of all each contributes a few coins to the common fund; and since the amount is seldom sufficient, then they select two or three men, whom they depute as their representatives to solicit contributions in the cities and villages from their fellow citizens, both Catholics and Protestants. When they have once collected enough money, then they buy a large enough tract of land upon which to build a church and priest house and to have a cemetery. However, when they have once decided to buy this tract, sometimes they hand over to the bishop the title of possession, so that he is the true possessor of this ecclesiastical property and is considered as such by the civil tribunals. But it often happens that the legislators of the province approach and obtain from them the title of possession, upon the condition that they transmit it to four or five Catholic men, who are elected annually by the congregation. In this case, these men are not only the temporal administrators of the temporalities of the church (*marguilliers*) as they are in Europe, but they have possession and are considered the true possessors of all the temporal goods of the church in the eyes of the civil tribunals and they can with impunity exercise over them the same authority as they do over their own homes and lands. However, a schism has never taken place in those churches, of which the bishop holds the civil title; in fact, it is impossible for it to happen there. For if the priest, who is constituted the pastor of this church, is addicted to drunkenness or impurity or other scandalous vices, and will not correct his life, then the bishop, by reason of the title he possesses, can at once remove him, just as any citizen has the right of expelling those who presume to occupy his home against his will. For he could easily obtain an order of eviction from the magistrates. But if the title of possession is in the hands of the temporal administrators (*marguilliers*), then they can easily raise the flag of rebellion against the bishop. If indeed the greater part of them do not fear God and conceive a hatred for their pastor, they will continually remove him from the church, no matter how great the sanctity of his life and customs; besides they deprive the entire Catholic congregation of the use of the church. . . .

READING NO. 12

THE CATHOLIC BISHOPS ON THE USE OF THE BIBLE, 1829*

Beginning in 1829, the American Catholic bishops gathered every few years to discuss common problems, assess the state of American Catholicism, and issue national pastoral letters to the clergy and laity in the country. Between 1829 and 1884, the bishops met ten times, thereby establishing a tradition of collegiality that continues to the present day. The resulting pastoral letters reflected the concerns of the bishops over the course of Church affairs. In these letters the bishops advised, admonished, and pleaded with the laity and the clergy to follow their lead. In the reading below, the bishops who gathered at the first Provincial Council of Baltimore in 1829 warned Catholics to use only the authorized Catholic version of the Bible.

γ   γ   γ

TEACHING ROLE OF THE BISHOPS

. . . 15. Deeming it therefore to be their most sacred duty, the bishops of the Church have scrupulously preserved unchanged through the innovation of time and the alterations of ages, the testimony of faith, and as a most precious portion thereof, the written word of God. Equally anxious to fulfill our important trust, we, too, desire to guard you against mistake and error. We, therefore, earnestly caution you against the indiscriminate use of unauthorized versions [of the Bible], for unfortunately many of those which are placed within your reach are extremely erroneous and defective. The Douay translation from the Vulgate of the Old Testament, together with the Rheims translation of the New Testament, are our

*Quoted from Hugh J. Nolan, ed., *Pastoral Letters of the U.S. Catholic Bishops* (Washington, 1984), vol. 1, pp. 43–44.

best English versions; but as some printers have undertaken in these states, by their own authority, without our sanction, to print and publish editions which have not been submitted to our examination, we cannot hold ourselves responsible for the correctness of such copies. We trust that henceforth it will be otherwise. We would also desire to correct that irregularity by which prayer books and other works of devotion and instruction are produced from the press, in several instances, without authority or correction; some of the books thus published are rather occasions of scandal rather than of edification. We would entreat of you not to encourage such proceedings. . . .

READING NO. 13

ALEXIS DE TOCQUEVILLE ON AMERICAN CATHOLICISM IN 1835*

American Catholicism experienced rapid and constant change during the middle years of the nineteenth century. A tremendous influx of immigrants transformed American Catholicism from a small minority denomination into the largest church in the country and the once native-born denomination became overwhelmingly foreign-born. Such dramatic demographic shifts precipitated a series of crises not only for Catholic leaders, but also native Americans. Could these impoverished foreigners become patriotic productive Americans and still remain loyal to their Church? There was more than one way to respond to these questions. In the passage below, the French observer Alexis de Tocqueville assesses the state of American Catholicism on the eve of the major period of immigration in American history.

γ   γ   γ

. . . About fifty years ago Ireland began to pour a Catholic population into the United States; and on their part, the Catholics of America made proselytes, so that, at the present moment more than a million Christians professing the truths of the Church of Rome are to be found in the Union. These Catholics are faithful to the observances of their religion; they are fervent and zealous in the belief of their doctrines. Yet they constitute the most republican and the most democratic class in the United States. This fact may surprise the observer at first, but the cause of it may easily be discovered upon reflection.

I think that the Catholic religion has erroneously been regarded as the natural enemy of democracy. Among the various sects of Christians, Catholicism seems to me, on the contrary,

*Quoted from Alexis de Tocqueville, *Democracy in America* (New York, 1945), vol. 1, pp. 300–302.

to be one of the most favorable to equality of condition among men. In the Catholic Church the religious community is composed of only two elements; the priest and the people. The priest alone rises above the rank of his flock, and all below him are equal.

On doctrinal points the Catholic faith places all human capacities upon the same level; it subjects the wise and ignorant, the man of genius and the vulgar crowd, to the details of the same creed; it imposes the same observances upon the rich and the needy, it inflicts the same austerities upon the strong and the weak: it listens to no compromise with mortal man, but, reducing all the human race to the same standard, it confounds all the distinctions of society at the foot of the same altar, even as they are confounded in the sight of God. If Catholicism predisposes the faithful to obedience, it certainly does not prepare them for inequality; but the contrary may be said of Protestantism, which generally tends to make men independent more than to render them equal. Catholicism is like an absolute monarchy; if the sovereign be removed, all the other classes of society are more equal than in republics.

It has not infrequently occurred that the Catholic priest has left the service of the altar to mix with the governing powers of society and to take his place among the civil ranks of men. This religious influence has sometimes been used to secure the duration of that political state of things to which he belonged. Thus we have seen Catholics taking the side of aristocracy from a religious motive. But no sooner is the priesthood entirely separated from the government, as is the case in the United States, than it is found that no class of men is more naturally disposed than the Catholics to transfer the doctrine of the equality of condition into the political world.

If, then, the Catholic citizens of the United States are not forcibly led by the nature of their tenets to adopt democratic and republican principles, at least they are not necessarily opposed to them; and their social position, as well as their limited number, obliges them to adopt these opinions. Most of the Catholics are poor, and they have no chance of taking a part in the government unless it is open to all the citizens. They constitute a minority, and all rights must be respected in order to ensure to them the free exercise of their own privileges. These two causes induce them, even unconsciously, to adopt political doctrines which they would perhaps support with less zeal if they were rich and preponderant.

The Catholic clergy of the United States have never attempted to oppose this political tendency; but they seek rather to justify it. The Catholic priests in America have divided the intellectual world into two parts; in the one they place the doctrines of revealed religion, which they assent to without discussion; in the other they leave those political truths which they believe the Deity has left open to free inquiry. Thus the Catholics of the United States are at the same time the most submissive believers and the most independent citizens. . . .

READING NO. 14

PROVIDING FOR THE GERMAN CATHOLICS IN AMERICA, 1845*

The German Catholic immigrants to the United States found themselves isolated from the Catholic Church and from American society. These Germans were uneasy in a religion dominated by Irishman and a society dominated by the English-speaking. As a means of preserving both their religious faith and their cultural heritage, the Germans organized "national" parishes where the liturgy and other vital services were conducted in their native language. Although effective in maintaining ethnic culture, these ethnic parishes were a divisive force within the Church for more than a century. In the reading below, Father Boniface Wimmer, O.S.B., writes to his colleagues in Germany in search of more priests to staff these new national parishes in America.

γ   γ   γ

. . . As far as I know the only Religious in the strict sense of the word now found in America are the Jesuits and Redemptorists. The missionaries of the Middle Ages, the Benedictines, Dominicans and Franciscans are not yet represented in the New World, except by a few individuals who do not live in monasteries. The Jesuits devote their energies principally to teaching in colleges; their students are mostly from the higher classes of society and many of them belong to Protestant families. Many Jesuits are also doing excellent work among the Indians, and others have charge of congregations in cities near their colleges. But while they accomplish so much in their sphere of labors, they can do little for Germans, because few of them speak their language. The Redemptorists are doing noble work for our countrymen in the States: in cities and thickly settled country districts they have

---

*Quoted from Colman J. Barry, *Worship and Work: St. John's Abbey and University, 1856–1956* (Collegeville, Minn., 1956), pp. 346–347, 350–351.

large congregations, and also do what they can for others as travelling missionaries. Some secular priests likewise go about among the scattered Catholics doing good, but they naturally and necessarily concentrate in cities where there is a large Catholic population.

We see, therefore, that much is being done in America; very much, indeed, when we consider the small band of priests and the difficulties under which they labor. But as yet nothing has been done for the stability of the work, no provision has been made for an increase of German-speaking priests, to meet the growing demand for missionary laborers. It is not difficult to see that secular priests, whose labors extend over a district larger than a diocese, can do nothing to secure reinforcements to their own number. . . .

We must not stifle our feelings of patriotism. The Germans, we hear it often enough, lose their national character in the second or third generation, they also lose their language, because like a little rivulet they disappear in the mighty stream of the Anglo-American population in the States. Is this not humiliating for us Germans? Would this sad condition of affairs continue if here and there a German center were established, to which the stream of emigration from our country could be systematically directed, if German instruction and sermons were given by priests going forth from these centers, if German books, papers and periodicals were distributed among the people, if German boys could receive a German education and training, which would make themselves felt in wider circles?

Let us, therefore, no longer build air castles for our countrymen in America. Let us provide for their religious interests, then their domestic affairs will take care of themselves. Benedictine monasteries of the old style are the best means of checking the downward tendencies of our countrymen in social, political and religious matters. Let Jesuits and Redemptorists labor side by side with the Benedictines; there is room enough for all and plenty of work. If every Religious Order develops a healthy activity within its sphere, the result will be doubly sure and great. North America will no longer depend upon Europe for its spiritual welfare, and the day may come when America will repay us just as England, converted by the Benedictines, repaid the continent of Europe.

READING NO. 15

JOHN HUGHES ON AMERICAN CATHOLICISM IN 1858*

Who would lead the American Church was an open question in 1830. To be sure the Pope selected bishops to serve as the leaders of each diocese, but the will of the Vatican was not enough to merit the respect of many American Catholics. American bishops in the nineteenth century faced disobedient priests, rebellious laymen, interethnic rivalries, native hostility, abject poverty, and other problems that threatened their ability to lead. A significant number of bishops failed in their quest to be leaders, but others became powerful "chieftains" over their diocesan Catholic communities. Certainly no bishop was more powerful or influential than John Hughes, the fiery archbishop of New York. In the passage below, he discusses his role as bishop and "chief."

γ   γ   γ

. . . The increase of the Catholic people in the United States has been very great indeed. But I think an exaggerated idea of the Catholic population would result from the assumption that it was in proportion to the increase of the hierarchy. We have forty-six bishops. The Catholic population throughout the whole United States can scarcely exceed three million and a half. These are very unequally distributed. In many dioceses the Catholics are very few. The bishops throughout the interior, residing in their quiet towns or villages, are anxious to propagate the kingdom of Christ in all simplicity and mildness, without saying or doing any thing that would excite the enmities or opposition of the Protestants among whom they live. The same remark would apply to several of the episcopal sees established in cities of a populous and prosperous character. Now *my* lot was cast in the great metropolis of the

---

*Quoted in John R.G. Hassard, *The Life of the Most Reverend John Hughes, D.D.* (New York, 1866), p. 389.

whole country. My people were composed of representatives from almost all nations. They came under episcopal government in a new country, and in circumstances such as they had not been accustomed to in their own. It was necessary that they should be brought to coalesce as one Catholic flock. They were surrounded by many inducements to diverge from the unity of the Church, both in profession and in practice. Many snares were laid for them; and, under these circumstances, I found it expedient to adopt a mode of government resulting almost by necessity from the peculiarity of my position. I had to stand up among them as their bishop and chief; to warn them against the dangers that surrounded them; to contend for their rights as a religious community; to repel the spirit of faction among them; to convince their judgment by frequent explanations in regard to public and mixed questions; to encourage the timid, and sometimes to restrain the impetuous; in short, to knead them up into one dough, to be leavened by the spirit of Catholic faith and of Catholic union. Hardly any thing of this kind was either expedient or necessary in any other episcopal see within the United States. . . .

READING NO. 16

THE CATHOLIC BISHOPS ON THE TEMPTATIONS OF AMERICAN LIFE, 1866*

In 1866, in the wake of the bloodiest war in American history, the Catholic bishops of the United States gathered in a national council to heal the wounds that had resulted from Catholic fighting against Catholic. It was an extraordinary event because many denominations had been so badly divided that reunion was not possible. The Second Plenary Council was evidence that the American Catholic Church could overcome bitter regional differences to function once again as a national denomination. During the council the bishops clarified a number of theological issues and reemphasized their collegial role as leaders of the Church in the United States. In the passage below from their pastoral letter, the bishops warned the laity of the many temptations of American life.

γ   γ   γ

THE LAITY

31. We continue to have great consolation in witnessing the advance of religion throughout the various dioceses, as shown in the multiplication and improved architectural character of our churches, the increase of piety in the various congregations, and the numerous conversions of so many who have sacrificed early prejudices and every consideration of their temporal interests and human feelings at the shrine of Catholic truth. We must, however, in all candor say, that we cannot include all, or indeed the greater part of those who compose our flocks, in this testimony to fidelity and zeal. Too many of them, including not infrequently men otherwise of blameless lives, remain for years estranged from the sacraments of the Church, although they

*Quoted in Hugh J. Nolan, ed., *Pastoral Letters of the U.S. Catholic Bishops* (Washington, 1984), vol. 1, pp. 201–203.

attend the celebration of the divine mysteries, and listen to the preaching of God's word with an earnestness and attention in themselves deserving of all praise. There are, indeed, others who, carried away by the impulse of passion, and but too easily influenced by evil examples, oblige us to rank them, as we do, weeping, after the example of the apostle, among "the enemies of the cross of Christ, whose end is destruction; whose God is their belly; and whose glory is their shame; who mind earthly things." It is impossible to estimate the injury these unworthy Catholics, and especially those who are the slaves of intemperance and its consequent vices, inflict on the Church. In the minds of but too many uninformed and unreflecting persons, these evils are taken as the confirmation of early prejudices; and the name of God is blasphemed among the nations by reason of the evil acts of those who, whilst they bear the name of Catholics, bring disgrace on their religion by their evil lives. Willingly would we have avoided reference to this painful subject; but we are not without hope, that our solemn protest against the evils we deplore may diminish, if not entirely remove, the scandal which they occasion; and that our united remonstrance may not be unheeded by those for whom "we watch, having to render an account of their souls": that they may be roused from the fatal lethargy in which they live, and, by sincere repentance and the practice of every good work compatible with their condition, repair, in some measure, the scandals they have given and the injury they have inflicted on the Church, by the irregularity of their past lives.

32. In this connection, we consider it to be our duty to warn our people against those amusements which may easily become to them an occasion of sin, and especially against those fashionable dances, which, as at present carried on, are revolting to every feeling of delicacy and propriety, and are fraught with the greatest danger to morals. We would also warn them most solemnly against the great abuses which have sprung up in the matter of fairs, excursions, and picnics, in which, as too often conducted, the name of charity is made to cover up a multitude of sins. We forbid all Catholics from having anything to do with them, except when managed in accordance with the regulations of the ordinary, and under the immediate supervision of their respective pastors.

33. We have noticed, with the most sincere satisfaction and gratitude to God, the great increase among us of societies and associations, especially of those composed of young and middle-aged men, conducted in strict accordance with the principles of the Catholic religion, and with an immediate view to their own sanctification. We cannot but anticipate the most beneficial results to the cause of morality and religion from the conduct and example of those who thus combine together, to encourage one another in the frequentation of the sacraments, and in works of Christian charity. We urge their extension, and especially of the Society of St. Vincent de Paul and of Young Men's Catholic Associations, in all the dioceses and parishes of the country, not only as useful auxiliaries to the parochial clergy, in the care of the poor, and of destitute and vagrant children, but also as one of the most important means of diminishing the vices and scandals of which we have spoken.

READING NO. 17

THE CATHOLIC BISHOPS SPEAK OUT ON PAROCHIAL EDUCATION, 1884*

Parochial education was the preoccupation of the American Catholic bishops during the nineteenth century. For more than five decades the bishops used pastoral letters to call upon the laity to support parochial schools, but with only limited success. To be sure, a great many Catholics did support parish schools, but more than half of the Catholic parents resisted the repeated pleas of the bishops. At the Third Plenary Council of Baltimore in 1884, the bishops changed their language from exhortation to command. They decreed that every parish would have a school within two years and that all parents should make a serious effort to send their children to that school. Although the tone of the passage below is pastoral, the message is clear—Catholics were to support parochial schools.

γ　　　　　γ　　　　　γ

EDUCATION AND RELIGION

. . . 32. Hence education, in order to foster civilization, must foster religion. Now the three great educational agencies are the home, the Church, and the school. These mold men and shape society. Therefore, each of them, to do its part well, must foster religion. But many, unfortunately, while avowing that religion should be the light and the atmosphere of the home and of the Church, are content to see it excluded from the school, and even advocate as the best school system that which necessarily excludes religion. Few surely will deny that childhood and youth are the periods of life when the character ought especially to be subjected to religious influences.

*Quoted in Hugh J. Nolan, ed., *Pastoral Letters of the U.S. Catholic Bishops* (Washington, 1984), vol. 1, pp. 224–225.

Nor can we ignore the palpable fact that the school is an important factor in the forming of childhood and youth—so important that its influence often outweighs that of home and Church. It cannot, therefore, be desirable or advantageous that religion should be excluded from the school. On the contrary, it ought, therefore, to be one of the chief agencies for molding the young life to all that is true and virtuous, and holy. To shut religion out of the school, and keep it for home and the Church, is, logically, to train up a generation that will consider religion good for home and the Church, but not for the practical business of real life. But a more false and pretentious notion could not be imagined. Religion, in order to elevate a people, should inspire their whole life and rule their relations with one another. A life is not dwarfed, but ennobled by being lived in the presence of God. Therefore, the school, which principally gives the knowledge fitting for practical life, ought to be pre-eminently under the holy influence of religion. From the shelter of home and school, the youth must soon go out into the busy ways of trade or traffic or professional practice. In all these, the principles of religion should animate and direct him. But he cannot expect to learn these principles in the workshop or the office or the counting-room. Therefore, let him be well and thoroughly imbued with them by the joint influences of home and school, before he is launched out on the dangerous sea of life.

33. All denominations of Christians are now awakening to this great truth, which the Catholic Church has never ceased to maintain. Reason and experience are forcing them to recognize that the only practical way to secure a Christian people, is to give the youth a Christian education. The avowed enemies of Christianity in some European countries are banishing religion from the schools, in order gradually to eliminate it from among the people. In this they are logical, and we may well profit by the lesson. Hence, the cry for Christian education is going up from all religious bodies throughout the land. And this is no narrowness and ''sectarianism'' on their part; it is an honest and logical endevor to preserve Christian truth and morality among the people by fostering religion in the young. Nor is it any antagonism to the state; on the contrary, it is an honest endeavor to give to the state better citizens, by making

them better Christians. The friends of Christian education do not condemn the state for not imparting religious instruction in the public schools as they are now organized; because they well know it does not lie within the province of the state to teach religion. They simply follow their conscience by sending their students to denominational schools, where religion can have its rightful place and influence.

34. Two objects, therefore, dear brethren, we have in view, to multiply our schools, and to perfect them. We must multiply them, till every Catholic child in the land shall have within his reach the means of education. There is still much to do ere this be attained. There are still thousands of Catholic children in the United States deprived of the benefit of a Catholic school. Pastors and parents should not rest till this defect be remedied. No parish is complete till it has schools adequate to the needs of its children, and the pastor and people of such a parish should feel that they have not accomplished their entire duty until the want is supplied.

35. But then, we must also perfect our schools. We repudiate the idea that the Catholic school need be in any respect inferior to any other school whatsoever. And if hitherto, in some places, our people have acted on the principle that it is better to have an imperfect Catholic school than to have none, let them now push their praiseworthy ambitions still further, and not relax their efforts till their schools be elevated to the highest educational excellence. And we implore parents not to hasten to take their children from school, but to give them all the time and all the advantages that they have the capacity to profit by, so that, in after life, their children may "rise up and call them blessed."

READING NO. 18

JAMES GIBBONS DEFENDS THE KNIGHTS OF LABOR, 1887*

One of the major issues faced by the American Catholic bishops at the end of the nineteenth century was the unionization of labor. Many of the men involved in organizing unions in the 1880s were Catholics as were the workers themselves. Should the Church condemn unions or were they a legitimate mechanism for defending the rights of workers? The Catholic bishops found themselves in the middle of the issue. Assured that the Knights of Labor, the largest union in the United States, was not a secret society, the majority of the archbishops voted against condemning the union. To insure that the Vatican would sustain this position, the newly consecrated Cardinal Archbishop of Baltimore, James Gibbons, sent the following letter to the Pope.

γ   γ   γ

. . . "It is of the United States that we speak, and we trust that we are not presumptuous in believing that we are competent to judge about the state of things in our own country. Now, as I have already indicated, out of the seventy-five archbishops and bishops of the United States, there are about five who desire the condemnation of the Knights of Labor, such as they are in our own country; so that our hierarchy are almost unanimous in protesting against such a condemnation. Such a fact ought to have great weight in deciding the question. If there are difficulties in the case, it seems to me that the prudence and experience of our bishops and the wise rules of the Third Plenary Council ought to suffice for their solution.

"Finally, to sum up all, it seems to me that the Holy See could not decide to condemn an association under the following circumstances:

---

*Quoted in Aaron Abell, ed., *American Catholic Thought on Social Questions* (New York, 1968), pp. 160–161.

156

"1. When the condemnation does not seem to be justified either by the letter or the spirit of its constitution, its law and the declaration of its chiefs.

"2. When the condemnation does not seem necessary, in view of the transient form of the organization and the social condition of the United States.

"3. When it does not seem to be prudent, because of the reality of the grievances complained of by the working classes, and their acknowledgement by the American people.

"4. When it would be dangerous for the reputation of the Church in our democratic country, and might even lead to persecution.

"5. When it would probably be inefficacious, owing to the general conviction that it would be unjust.

"6. When it would be destructive instead of beneficial in its effects, impelling the children of the Church to disobey their Mother, and even to enter condemned societies, which they have thus far shunned.

"7. When it would turn into suspicion and hostility the singular devotedness of our Catholic people towards the Holy See.

"8. When it would be regarded as a cruel blow to the authority of the bishops in the United States, who, it is well known, protest against such a condemnation.

"Now, I hope the considerations here presented have sufficiently shown that such would be the effect of condemnation of the Knights of Labor in the United States.

"Therefore, I leave the decision of the case, with fullest confidence to the wisdom and prudence of your Eminence and the Holy See."

READING NO. 19

JOHN IRELAND DEFENDS THE PUBLIC SCHOOLS, 1890*

The major conflict within the Catholic hierarchy in the late nineteenth century was over education. All of these men— liberals as well as conservatives—agreed that Catholic schooling was a necessity if Catholicism was to flourish in America. Beyond that simple commitment, however, these men could agree on little else. Conflict ensued when Archbishop John Ireland of St. Paul proposed a plan for schools in select American communities to be administered jointly by church and state. The uproar caused by the plan was heard across the country and all the way to Rome. The controversy raged throughout 1891 and 1892 with no sign of abating. To end it all the Pope had to issue a statement on the matter. In the letter that follows, Archbishop Ireland defends his plan.

γ　　　　　γ　　　　　γ

. . . My appeal for State Schools fit for Catholic children has been censured under the plea that a Protestant state should touch nothing Catholic. But America is not a "Protestant State," and if Catholics pay school taxes they should receive benefit from them. The burden upon our Catholics to maintain parish schools up to the required standard for all the children of the Church is almost unbearable. There is danger that never shall we have schools for all Catholic children, or that Catholics will grow tired of contributing. At present nearly half the Catholic children of America do not attend parish-schools. The true solution, in my judgment, is to make the State-School satisfactory to Catholic consciences, and to use it. Can this be done? Let us try. If it cannot be done, let us do our best with our parish-schools.

Besides have not bishops and priests gone too far in their

*Quoted in Daniel P. Reilly, *The School Controversy, 1891–1893,* (Washington, 1943), pp. 239–240.

denunciations of the State School? Have they not, in their desire to protect the parish school, often belied, in their exaggerations of the evil, the State School? Have they not gone beyond the ''Apostolic Instruction'' of 1875? Have they not needlessly brought upon us the odium of the country? Indeed, since our own schools are neither numerous enough, nor efficient enough for our children, and many of these must attend the public school, have we not done immense harm to souls by our anathemas? Catholics in many cases must use those schools, and yet they are denounced for it; their consciences are falsified—they are estranged from the Church. I am not afraid to say that in places where bishops have been very severe against Public schools, their parish schools have done more harm than good to religion.

It is well, too, to remark that our public schools, in many places at least, are not *positively* bad. They are not hot beds of vice; neither do they teach unbelief or Protestantism. Teachers are often good Catholics; or at least they are gentlemen or ladies, decorous in conduct, and generous toward our faith. I know well the immense advantage to children of positive dogmatic teaching in school; yet, where the school is as nearly neutral as can be—the family and the Sunday School can do much—tho' never all we should give if circumstances permit.. . . .

I have myself no further remarks to make. If fault were to be found in Rome with the address, let the precise point with which fault is found be quickly pointed out to me and I will give explanation, or if necessary quietly withdraw it. A public condemnation from Rome of the address would set America in fury, as it would be a direct attack on principles which America will not give up, that is the right of the State to provide for the instruction of all children. As I am so clear on the need of religion in the Schools, Rome's condemnation will be understood to bear on the fact that I allow any right to the State.

I repeat—I have read all the objections to the discourse, and they come either from partial reading of my words, or from hatred of the American state.. . . .

READING NO. 20

MARTIN DOOLEY ON THE OBSERVATION OF LENT, 1894*

Catholics enjoyed an occasional laugh at the foibles and pitfalls of Church liturgical practices. Among the most arduous duties faced by Catholics each year was to fast between meals and abstain from eating meat on selected days during Lent—the forty days between Ash Wednesday and Easter. Catholics also were encouraged—even expected—to give up their vices during Lent. For some Catholics that meant no smoking, no drinking, no gambling, and no swearing. In the passage below, "Martin J. Dooley," a fictitious Irish Catholic saloonkeeper in Chicago, complains to a friend about the burden on being a Catholic during Lent. Dooley was the creation of Finley Peter Dunne, a Chicago journalist at the turn of the century. Dunne and Dooley went on to become national celebrities during the first three decades of the twentieth century.

γ   γ   γ

"Well, thin," said Mr. Dooley, "thank hivin that Lint is almost over, Gawd f'rgive me f'r sayin' it. 'Tis very thryin' on the soul—not th' fastin', mind ye; but th' thought, bedad, that ye shud be fastin' whin ye aren't. I suppose, Mr. McKinna, that ye'd think nothing iv tuckin' in a slab iv beef on Good Friday, like anny prowtestant, but f'r me an' th' likes iv me, 'tis different. If I was to ate meat this blessed day I'd go th' way Hinnissy's goat wint that thried to di-gest th' hoopskirt. I'd choke to death on that there flure.

"Whin Ash Whin'sday come around I says to mesilf, I says: 'Ma-artin,' I says, 'ye've not been on ye'er good behavior this year.' I says, 'an 'twould be a good thing f'r ye to put in this here holy season of Lint,' I says, 'squarin' ye'erself,' I

*Quoted in Charles Fanning, ed., *Mr. Dooley and the Chicago Irish* (New York, 1976), pp. 80–82.

says, 'be fastin' an abstainin.' So, thinks I, I'll stop off swearin', drinkin', smokin' and playin' ca-ards till afther Easter. Well, sir, I done all right through th' wan day, though I was dam dhry f'r a smoke afther me dinner. But th' nixt day, whin I was goin' by th' gashouse, I cracked me shin again a skid an' forgettin' me good intintions I swore till half the women along th' road begun to call in their childher. Iv coorse I had to scratch off swearin' an' thry to play th' shtring out with th' other three. I done all right through th' afthernoon, but at night that big Clare man, O'Toole, he come in. I don't like a hair iv his head an' he knows it, so I says, 'Terence,' I says, 'I'm glad to see ye.'

" 'How ar-re ye?' says he. 'I was goin' by,' he says, 'an' I thought I'd come in an' play ye a little game iv forty-fives.' ' 'Tis Lint,' says I. ' 'Tis a good excuse,' says he. 'What's that?' says I. 'Oh,' he says, with a laugh, 'I don't blame ye,' he says, with that mane smile iv his. 'I don't blame ye,' he says. 'There's very few min fr'm ye'er part iv Connack that can play games,' he says, 'that ray-quires intillegence,' he says. 'Ye'er betther a long way at pitchin' quates,' he says. I was hoppin' mad in a minyet. Says I: 'There niver was a man born in th' County Clare,' says I, 'that could bate me playin' forty-fives,' I says. 'Come on,' says I. 'What for?' says he. 'Th' dhrinks,' says I. 'An' th' see-gars,' says he. 'It's a go,' says I, an' there I was, all me good intintions down at wanst. 'Twas a judgment on him f'r challengin' me that he lost tin straight games an' had to walk clear to Brighton f'r lack iv car fare.

"An' mind ye, whin a man swears off annything, Jawn, an' falls down wanst, 'tis all over. He goes in deeper than iver, an' be hivins I've done ivrything bad this here Lint but th' wan thing. I've et no meat on a fast day, and 'tis a ha-ard shtrain upon a ma-an like me."

At this moment the boy from Clancy's restaurant came in to find what Mr. Dooley wanted brought over for dinner.

"Mickey," said Mr. Dooley, "tell ye'er father to cuk that big fish I seen in th' window, an' some soft biled eggs, an' some sparrygrass an' a dish uv coffee. Hell-an'-all, I wish Lint was over."

READING NO. 21

IMMIGRANT PARISH LIFE IN CHICAGO IN 1905*

The parish had been the focal point of American Catholic religious life since the end of the eighteenth century. The millions of Catholics who arrived annually after 1820 intensified Catholic religious life at the local level by establishing "national parishes"—self-contained ethnic ghettos that preserved Old World traditions and customs. These national parishes would be a vibrant, though controversial, institution in American Catholicism for more than a century. In the passage below, a visiting Catholic bishop from Hungary describes the dedication of a new church and rectory in Our Lady of Hungary parish in Chicago.

γ   γ   γ

. . . More than half the population of Chicago are foreigners. . . . There are over 200,000 Italians, and the Hungarians proper, not included in other categories, must be estimated at nearly 15,000 new arrivals within the last few years. These latter are chiefly employed as butchers in the slaughterhouses, and as blacksmiths and carpenters in the Pullman establishment. It was at the expense of these people that the little church was built which now met my view. It stands like a beacon amid the surrounding marshes; it is the nucleus of a new suburb, which will spring up around it, and will certainly be no less important a part of the metropolis than the others which have arisen at 16 miles from the centre of the town. It is a first step towards progress, another foundation stone of civilisation and culture.

The workmen and their families awaited me at the entrance of the building. For the greater part they were still dressed in their simple costume "from over the sea," and their whole

*Quoted in John Tracy Ellis, ed., *Documents of American Catholic History* (Milwaukee, 1956), pp. 572–574.

demeanour showed that they had not long since arrived in these parts. Set adrift in that great city, without knowing the language, without friends or any one to advise them, these poor folks are at the mercy of chance. And, in addition to all the other difficulties and problems which the municipal authorities have to face, we can well understand that this question of dealing with the foreign population of inferior civilisation is one of the greatest and hardest to solve. They have not only to be fed, they have also to be protected and educated. The church and the school are their only safeguards. As long as the people will go to church and are willing to have their children brought up on religious principles there is nothing to fear. As long as they recognise their duty towards God they will also recognise and fulfil their duty towards their neighbour.

The inauguration of that humble little church and its simple worshippers has left an indelible impression upon me. It was one of those never-to-be-forgotten scenes which, in spite of their apparent unimportance, form a page in the annals of history. This small beginning, representing the accumulated savings of those hardy workmen, is the centre of new efforts and new struggles. Let us hope these may lead here to as successful an issue as they have done in other parts of the town. Let us hope that its inhabitants may one day be as prosperous and wealthy as their fellow-citizens in older Chicago. Above all, let us hope that the little church may grow into a cathedral, and its elementary school into a great scientific establishment. And although in the past the place has so often been shaken by strikes and tumults, let us hope that henceforth faith and culture may ensure peace and prosperity to this marvellous city. . . .

Our church, a modest wooden building of two stories, used also as a school and as a habitation of the priest, rises like a landmark in the midst of a desert of factories, for here are the ironworks of the Illinois Steel Trust, and the famous workshops of the Pullman Car Company. In both of these great enterprises the number of hands employed greatly exceeds 10,000, drawn for the most part from Austro-Hungary. That is why this parish was formed. The population, called into existence by these works, required the consolations of religion, and their numerous progeny needed education and care, in an atmosphere impregnated with smoke and alcohol.

When at last I arrived, after a long journey, I found the church crammed with workmen and their families, all persons who earned their daily bread by the sweat of their brow. This sympathetic crowd, and the warmth of their reception, almost made me forget that the congregation had gathered in an erection made of planks, more like a barn than a place of worship.

What was my surprise at the end of my sermon when the priest appealed to the generosity of the worshippers, and, a sheet of paper in his hand, held a meeting of the congregation, asking them to furnish the empty building. The altar-cloth, ornaments—everything was subscribed with a truly Christian generosity, and if ever Providence should again take me back, I am certain that I should find that humble parish a most flourishing centre. . . .

READING NO. 22

THE CATHOLIC FOREIGN MISSION SOCIETY OF AMERICA, 1911*

Until 1908, the Vatican considered the United States a mission territory—not yet a mature national church to be allowed to administer its own affairs. Up until that date, other bishops of the world were encouraged to provide priests and nuns for the American missions. But by 1910, the American Church, with its more than sixteen million Catholics, had obtained a size that rivaled the Church in most nations of Europe. It was time for the American Church to send missionaries to other, less fortunate nations. The establishment of the Catholic Foreign Mission Society in March 1911 marked the beginning of this effort. The CFMS became known as "Maryknoll" after the site of its seminary in New York, and for the next four decades sent thousands of young men and women around the globe. Indeed, when the American mission movement reached its peak in the 1950s, nearly 5000 young Americans were serving in Catholic religious orders outside the United States. The passage below is from the document establishing the Maryknoll order.

γ   γ   γ

At the request of His Excellency, the Apostolic Delegate, I submit to your consideration a plan to establish an American Foreign Mission Seminary.

That such a Seminary is needed, and urgently, seems daily more evident. The prestige of our country has become widespread; and Protestants, especially in the Far East, are profiting by it, to the positive hindrance of Catholic missioners. I understand that even the educated classes in China, misled by the almost complete absence of American Catholic priests,

*Quoted in John Tracy Ellis, ed., *Documents of American Catholic History* (Milwaukee, 1956), pp. 592–593.

believe that the Church of Rome has no standing in America. . . .

The priests of the United States number more than 17,000 but I am informed that there are hardly sixteen on the foreign missions. This fact recalls a warning which the late Cardinal Vaughan gave in a kindly and brotherly letter addressed to me nearly twenty-two years ago, urging us American Catholics not to delay participation in foreign missions, LEST OUR OWN FAITH SHOULD SUFFER.

We must confess that as a Catholic body we have only begun, while our Protestant fellow-countrymen have passed the century mark in foreign mission work and are represented today in the heathen world by some thousands of missioners, who are backed by yearly contributions running up into the millions.

A seminary, such as that contemplated, if established with the good-will of the entire American Hierarchy, can hardly fail to draw, emphatically, the attention of American Catholics.

"It is time," to use the words of the Apostolic Delegate, "that the American Church should begin to move in this direction." . . .

READING NO. 23

THE BISHOPS' PROGRAM OF SOCIAL RECONSTRUCTION, 1919*

Among the most powerful and important statements issued by the American Catholic bishops was Social Reconstruction: A General View of the Problems and a Survey of the Remedies. *Published in the aftermath of World War I, this statement looked toward the establishment of a more democratic American society in which labor, management, and government worked together for a common good. At the time the bishops' proposals were issued, they were branded as socialism and largely rejected. Yet ten of the eleven proposals were eventually incorporated in the Democratic programs of Franklin D. Roosevelt and his successors. The statement had originated with Father John A. Ryan, author of* The Living Wage *(1906) and the leading Catholic social thinker of his day. The bishops were so impressed with Ryan's work on* Social Reconstruction *that they gave their endorsement to it as a pastoral statement. Ryan later served as a liaison between the bishops and the Roosevelt administration.*

γ   γ   γ

FUNDAMENTAL REFORMS

. . . 34. It seems clear that the present industrial system is destined to last for a long time in its main outlines. That is to say, private ownership of capital is not likely to be supplanted by a collectivist organization of industry at a date sufficiently near to justify any present action based on the hypothesis of its arrival. This forecast we recognize as not only extremely probable, but as highly desirable; for, other objections apart,

*Quoted in Hugh J. Nolan, ed., *Pastoral Letters of the U.S. Catholic Bishop*, 4 vols., (Washington, D.C., 1984), 1:268–271. Used by permission of the U.S. Catholic Conference.

Socialism would mean bureaucracy, political tyranny, the helplessness of the individual as a factor in the ordering of his own life, and in general social inefficiency and decadence.

DEFECTS OF PRESENT SYSTEM

35. Nevertheless, the present system stands in grievous need of considerable modifications and improvement. Its main defects are three: Enormous inefficiency and waste in the production and distribution of commodities; insufficient incomes for the great majority of wage-earners, and unnecessarily large incomes for a small minority of privileged capitalists. Inefficiency in the production and distribution of goods would be in great measure abolished by the reforms that have been outlined in the foregoing pages. Production would be greatly increased by universal living wages, by adequate industrial education, and by harmonious relations between labor and capital on the basis of adequate participation by the former in all the industrial aspects of business management. The wastes of commodity distribution could be practically all eliminated by co-operative mercantile establishments, and co-operative selling and marketing associations.

CO-PARTNERSHIP

36. Nevertheless, the full possibilities of increased production will not be realized so long as the majority of the workers remain mere wage-earners. The majority must somehow become owners, or at least in part, of the instruments of production. They can be enabled to reach this stage gradually through co-operative productive societies and co-partnership arrangements. In the former, the workers own and manage the industries themselves; in the latter they own a substantial part of the corporate stock and exercise a reasonable share in the management. However slow the attainments of these ends, they will have to be reached before we can have a thoroughly efficient system of production, or an industrial and social order that will be secure from the danger of revolution. It is to

be noted that this particular modification of the existing order, though far-reaching and involving to a great extent the abolition of the wage system, would not mean the abolition of private ownership. The instruments of production would still be owned by individuals, not by the State.

INCREASED INCOMES

37. The second great evil, that of insufficient income for the majority can be removed only by providing the workers with more income. This means not only universal living wages, but the opportunity of obtaining something more than that amount for all who are willing to work hard and faithfully. All the other measures for labor betterment recommended in the preceding pages would likewise contribute directly or indirectly to a more just distribution of wealth in the interest of the laborer.

NEW SPIRIT NEEDED

38. For the third evil mentioned above, excessive gains by a small minority of privileged capitalists, the main remedies are prevention of monopolistic control of commodities, adequate government regulation of such public service monopolies as will remain under private operation, and heavy taxation of incomes, excess profits and inheritances. The precise methods by which genuine competition may be restored and maintained among businesses that are naturally competitive, cannot be discussed here; but the principle is clear that human beings cannot be trusted with the immense opportunities for oppression and extortion that go with the possession of monopoly power. That the owners of public service monopolies should be restricted by law to a fair or average return on their actual investment, has long been a recognized principle of the courts, the legislatures, and public opinion. It is a principle which should be applied to competitive enterprises likewise, with the qualification that something more than the average rate of return should be allowed to men who exhibit exceptional effi-

ciency. However, good public policy, as well as equity, demands that these exceptional business men share the fruits of their efficiency with the consumer in the form of lower prices. The man who utilizes his ability to produce cheaper than his competitors for the purpose of exacting from the public as high a price for his product as is necessary for the least efficient business man, is a menace rather than a benefit to industry and society.

Our immense war debt constitutes a particular reason why incomes and excess profits should continue to be heavily taxed. In this way two important ends will be attained: the poor will be relieved of injurious tax burdens, and the small class of specially privileged capitalists will be compelled to return a part of their unearned gains to society. . . .

A CHRISTIAN VIEW

40. "Society," said Pope Leo XIII, "can be healed in no other way than by a return to Christian life and Christian institutions." The truth of these words is more widely perceived to-day than when they were written, more than twenty-seven years ago. Changes in our economic and political systems will have only partial and feeble efficiency if they be not reinforced by the Christian view of work and wealth. Neither the moderate reforms advocated in this paper, nor any other program of betterment or reconstruction will prove reasonably effective without a reform in the spirit of both labor and capital. The laborer must come to realize that he owes his employer and society an honest day's work in return for a fair wage, and that conditions cannot be substantially improved until he roots out the desire to get a maximum of return for a minimum of service. The capitalist must likewise get a new viewpoint. He needs to learn the long-forgotten truth that wealth is stewardship, that profit-making is not the basic justification of business enterprise, and that there are such things as fair profits, fair interest and fair prices. Above and before all, he must cultivate and strengthen within his mind the truth which many of his class have begun to grasp for the first time during the present war; namely, that the laborer is a human

being, not merely an instrument of production; and that the laborer's right to a decent livelihood is the first moral charge upon industry. The employer has a right to get a reasonable living out of his business, but he has no right to interest on his investment until his employees have obtained at least living wages. This is the human and Christian, in contrast to the purely commercial and pagan, ethics of industry.

READING NO. 24

THE SUPREME COURT AND THE RIGHTS OF PAROCHIAL SCHOOLS, 1925*

What was the proper relationship between church, state, and school in the United States? That question had been asked repeatedly throughout the nineteenth century without resolution. There seemed to be no end to the controversy. In the 1920s, during a period of intense nativism, the state of Oregon proposed to address the issue by abolishing private schools. Not surprisingly, Catholics and other religious groups fought back, arguing that the state had no authority to usurp the rights of parents to decide on the education of their children. The case, Pierce v. Society of Sisters, *was appealed all the way to the Supreme Court. In a brief, unanimous decision, the Court struck down the Oregon law and upheld the constitutionality of private and religious education. The decision is considered by many to be the "Magna Carta" of American Catholic education.*

γ   γ   γ

. . . No question is raised concerning the power of the State reasonably to regulate all schools, to inspect, supervise and examine them, their teachers and pupils; to require that all children of proper age attend some school, that teachers shall be of good moral character and patriotic disposition, that certain studies plainly essential to good citizenship must be taught, and that nothing be taught which is manifestly inimical to the public welfare.

The inevitable practical result of enforcing the Act under consideration would be destruction of appellees' primary schools, and perhaps all other private primary schools for normal children within the State of Oregon. Appellees are engaged in a kind of undertaking not inherently harmful, but long regarded as useful and meritorious. Certainly there is

*Quoted in *Pierce v. Society of Sisters,* 268 U.S. 510.

nothing in the present records to indicate that they have failed to discharge their obligations to patrons, students, or the State. And there are no peculiar circumstances or present emergencies which demand extraordinary measures relative to primary education.

Under the doctrine of *Meyer v. Nebraska,* 262 U.S. 390, we think it entirely plain that the Act of 1922 unreasonably interferes with the liberty of parents and guardians to direct the upbringing and education of children under their control. As often heretofore pointed out rights guaranteed by the Constitution may not be abridged by legislation which has no reasonable relation to some purpose within the competency of the State. The fundamental theory of liberty upon which all governments in this Union repose excludes any general power of the State to standardize its children by forcing them to accept instruction from public teachers only. The child is not the mere creature of the State; those who nurture him and direct his destiny have the right, coupled with the high duty, to recognize and prepare him for additional obligations. . . .

READING NO. 25

AL SMITH DEFENDS HIS RELIGIOUS BELIEFS, 1928*

Another question commonly asked in the 1920s was whether a Catholic could serve as President of the United States. How could any man serve two masters—the Catholic Church and the U.S. Constitution? The question was a serious issue at the 1924 and 1928 Democratic National Conventions when Governor Alfred E. Smith of New York was nominated for the presidency. As the Democratic party's nominee in 1928, Smith faced a panoply of outrageous accusations, particularly that he was a tool of the Vatican. Smith repeatedly stressed his commitment to the separation of church and state, but to little avail. He was defeated by Herbert Hoover in a vicious, bitter campaign. In the passage below, Smith attacks religious prejudice and notes his own commitment to American principles.

γ   γ   γ

. . . I can think of no greater disaster to this country than to have the voters of it divide upon religious lines. It is contrary to the spirit, not only of the Declaration of Independence, but of the Constitution itself. During all of our national life we have prided ourselves throughout the world on the declaration of the fundamental American truth that all men are created equal.

Our forefathers, in their wisdom, seeing the danger to the country of a division on religious issues, wrote into the Constitution of the United States in no uncertain words the declaration that no religious test shall ever be applied for public office, and it is a sad thing in 1928, in view of the countless billions of dollars that we have poured into the cause of public education, to see some American citizens proclaiming them-

*Quoted in *Campaign Addresses of Governor Alfred E. Smith* (Washington, 1929), pp. 49, 51, 58.

selves 100 per cent American, and in the document that makes that proclamation suggesting that I be defeated for the presidency because of my religious belief.

The Grand Dragon of the Realm of Arkansas, writing to a citizen of that State, urges my defeat because I am Catholic, and in the letter suggests to the man, who happened to be a delegate to the Democratic convention, that by voting against me he was upholding American ideals and institutions as established by our forefathers.

The Grand Dragon that thus advised a delegate to the national convention to vote against me because of my religion is a member of an order known as the Ku Klux Klan, who have the effrontery to refer to themselves as 100 per cent Americans.

Yet totally ignorant of the history and tradition of this country and its institutions and, in the name of Americanism, they breathe into the hearts and souls of their members hatred of millions of their fellow countrymen because of their religious belief. . . .

One of the things, if not the meanest thing, in the campaign is a circular pretending to place someone of my faith in the position of seeking votes for me because of my Catholicism. Like everything of this kind, of course it is unsigned, and it would be impossible to trace its authorship. It reached me through a member of the Masonic order who, in turn, received it in the mail. It is false in its every line. It was designed on its very face to injure me with members of churches other than my own.

I here emphatically declare that I do not wish any member of my faith in any part of the United States to vote for me on any religious grounds. I want them to vote for me only when in their hearts and consciences they become convinced that my election will promote the best interests of our country.

By the same token, I cannot refrain from saying that any person who votes against me simply because of my religion is not, to my way of thinking, a good citizen. . . .

The constitutional guaranty that there should be no religious test for public office is not a mere form of words. It represents the most vital principle that ever was given any people.

I attack those who seek to undermine it, not only because I am a good Christian, but because I am a good American and a product of America and of American institutions. Everything I am, and everything I hope to be, I owe to these institutions.

The absolute separation of State and Church is part of the fundamental basis of our Constitution. I believe in that separation, and in all that it implies. That belief must be a part of the fundamental faith of every true American. . . .

READING NO. 26

CHARLES COUGHLIN ATTACKS THE ROOSEVELT ADMINISTRATION, 1935*

Even though the majority of American Catholics were avid supporters of Franklin D. Roosevelt and the New Deal, one of the most powerful and influential Catholics in America was not—Father Charles E. Coughlin, who rose to fame and influence through the power of the radio. Beginning with a local show in Detroit in the late 1920s, Coughlin enlarged his audience each year because of his ability to capture succinctly the material and spiritual concerns of millions of Americans, both Catholic and non-Catholic. By the early 1930s his show was broadcast nationwide and Coughlin had to employ 100 secretaries to answer his mail.

During the early 1930s, Coughlin was an active supporter of the New Deal. But the Roosevelt administration did not move quickly enough for Coughlin and he became increasingly critical of the President and his policies. He eventually broke with the Democrats altogether and joined other critics in forming a third political party in 1936. Coughlin's influence waned after 1936 as his weekly sermons took on pro-fascist and anti-Semitic overtones. He was silenced by his bishop in the early 1940s; he was an embarrassment to American Catholicism. In the news story below, Coughlin announces his break with Roosevelt.

γ   γ   γ

DETROIT, Nov. 17 (AP).—The Rev. Charles E. Coughlin, who began to turn a mildly critical fire on the Washington scene two years ago, ran up his battle flags today as a foe of the Roosevelt administration policies.

Declaring that the principles of the New Deal and those of his own widespread following, the National Union for Social

*Quoted in *The New York Times*, (November 18, 1935).

Justice, "are unalterably opposed," Father Coughlin completed his break with the administration on questions involving money, labor and agriculture.

When the Roosevelt administration entered the White House, Father Coughlin supported the President, and coined the slogan: "Roosevelt or Ruin."

"On March 4, 1933, I was thrilled to the ringing words which promised to drive the money changers from the temple," he said today in his Sunday afternoon broadcast over a national hook-up.

"I thought that the death-knell for plutocracy had sounded.

"Today I humbly stand before the American public to admit that I have been in error. Despite all promises, the money changer has not been driven from the temple."

He described his address today as an accounting of his stewardship of the National Union for Social Justice which he organized two years ago and for which he now claims 9,000,000 membership applications.

Father Coughlin charged the New Deal with supporting two extremes, "communistic tendencies" and the "error plutocracy."

The administration, he said, supported a "slave wage" and not a living wage in its work relief programs. The Agricultural Adjustment Administration policies, he said, only "deceived the farmer with the hypodermic needle of the dole." He characterized the AAA as "economic hoaxing," and a "clever wedge between city and farm."

Discussing the Congressional enactment of labor legislation, including the NRA, Father Coughlin said:

"Did not the Presidential Advisers recognize that the NRA was unconstitutional?"

These facts impel me to suspect that the labor legislation enacted by this government was another phase of a sham battle to protect plutocracy at the expense of the Supreme Court's prestige."

READING NO. 27

DOROTHY DAY AND THE CATHOLIC WORKER MOVEMENT, 1939*

One of the most important and lasting social action movements of the 1930s was the Catholic Worker movement. Begun in May 1933 by the American journalist Dorothy Day and the French social philosopher Peter Maurin, the Catholic Worker was a bit of everything—a social philosophy, a newspaper, a consortium of hospitality houses, and above all, a catalyst for change within the Church. Even though Maurin was the philosopher of the movement, Day was the driving force behind the Catholic Worker. It was Day who kept the newspaper going, and it was Day who saw to the urban hospitality houses and the farming communes. Most of all, it was Day's charisma or "presence," as one worker called it, that shaped two generations of Catholic activists. In the passage below, Day provides a brief overview of the philosophy of the Catholic Worker movement.

γ   γ   γ

. . . We have never faltered in our conviction during these six years of work that hospices such as our Houses of Hospitality are a vital necessity in times like these.

We do not deny that the State is bound for the sake of the common good, to take care of the unemployed and the unemployable by relief and lodging houses and work projects. Pope Pius XI pointed that out very clearly. He lamented that so much money was spent in increased armaments that should be spent on the poor. He urged the "press and the pulpit throughout the world" to fight the increase of armaments, and added sadly that "up to this time Our voice has not been heard."

No, we are not denying the obligations of the State. But we

*Quoted in Dorothy Day, *House of Hospitality* (New York, 1939), pp. 257–259. Used with the permission of Sheed & Ward, 115 E. Armour Blvd., Kansas City, MO.

do claim that we must never cease to emphasize personal responsibility. When our brother asks us for bread, we cannot say, "Go be thou filled." We cannot send him from agency to agency. We must care for him ourselves as much as possible.

And we claim that as Catholics we have not sufficiently cared for our own. We have not used the material, let alone the spiritual resources at our disposal. We have not drawn upon our tremendous reserves of material and spiritual wealth. We have scarcely known or recognized that we possessed them.

Approximately twenty-five million Catholics in the United States! It would be interesting to know how many of them are on relief, trusting to State aid. If we took care of our own, and relieved the government of this immediate responsibility, how conditions would be transformed! Then indeed people could say "See how they love one another!" Then indeed we would be "bearing one another's burdens." But of course, we would not be limiting our care only to our own. We would inevitably be caring also for others outside the faith.

This would also point the way to a solution of the industrial problem. As Christian masters freed the slaves who had converted them, because they recognized their dignity as men made in the image and likeness of God, so the industrial slaves of today can find freedom through Christianity.

Certainly this is an upside-down way of looking at the problem from a worldly standpoint. But we are fools for Christ's sake. We are the little ones God has chosen to confound the wise. We are the least of His children, yet through us He has done great things. Surely the simple fact of feeding five thousand people a day, in all our houses month after month for a number of years, is a most astounding proof that God loves our work. . . .

READING NO. 28

THE CATHOLIC BISHOPS ON VICTORY AND PEACE, 1942*

Many American Catholics differed with the Roosevelt administration on foreign policy. Like many Americans, Catholics tended to be isolationists. Roosevelt was not without Catholic supporters on foreign policy, of course, but the numbers were small. Yet as a group, Catholics were among the most loyal Americans; once war had been declared, Catholics eagerly joined the armed forces and served with distinction in Europe and in the Pacific. Catholics constituted between twenty-five and thirty-five percent of the armed forces during World War II, a percentage significantly higher than their percentage of the population. In the passage below from their pastoral letter of 1942, the Catholic bishops call upon all Catholics to join the war effort.

γ　　　　　γ　　　　　γ

1. Our country has been forced into the most devastating war of all time. This war, which is the absorbing interest of all the world, involves unquestionably the most important moral issue of today. Some nations are united in waging war to bring about a slave world—a world that would deprive man of his divinely conferred dignity, reject human freedom, and permit no religious liberty. We are associated with other powers in a deadly conflict against these nations to maintain a free world. This conflict of principles makes compromise impossible.

2. While war is the last means to which a nation should resort, circumstances arise when it is impossible to avoid it. At times it is the positive duty of a nation to wage war in the defense of life and right. Our country now finds itself in such circumstances.

*Quoted in Hugh J. Nolan, ed., *Pastoral Letters of the U.S. Catholic Bishops* (Washington, 1984), vol. 2, pp. 38–39. Used by permission of the U.S. Catholic Conference.

3. Even while we meet here, the exigencies of war have driven our armed forces into unexpected areas of conflict in Africa. Our president, in letters addressed to the rulers of all the friendly nations concerned, has given solemn assurance that the United States has no designs of permanent conquest or sordid interest. Our aim, he pledged, is to guarantee to countries under temporary occupation as well as to our own the right to live in security and peace. We bishops are confident that the pledge of our chief executive, not lightly made, faithfully mirrors the mind and conscience of the American people. That pledge is in full harmony with the expression of high purpose which the president made to the Catholic bishops of the United States when our own country was plunged into war: "We shall win this war and in victory we shall seek not vengeance but the establishment of an international order in which the spirit of Christ shall rule the hearts of men and nations."

4. From the moment that our country declared war we have called upon our people to make the sacrifices which, in Catholic doctrine, the virtues of patriotism, justice, and charity impose. In every section of this nation the voices of our bishops have been heard. Their instructions, their pastorals, their counsels, their appeals for prayers are an encouragement and an inspiration to their flocks. Our priests as chaplains on the war front have inspired confidence in the men whom they so zealously serve. Our men in the armed forces deserve unstinted gratitude for their heroic services to our country and high commendation for the faithful practice of their religion.

READING NO. 29

PAUL BLANSHARD ON AMERICAN FREEDOM AND CATHOLIC POWER, 1949*

The years after World War II saw an increase in tension between Catholics and other Americans. The violence and overt anti-Catholicism of previous generations were gone, but there was no shortage of vitriolic rhetoric. The arguments during these years focused on three issues—the continuing presence of the U.S. ambassador in the Vatican, the effort of Catholics to obtain public funds for parochial schools, and the organized Protestant response to Catholic involvement in public affairs. Among the most active and vocal critics of American Catholicism was Paul Blanshard, a former State Department employee turned free-lance writer. Blanshard published a number of critiques of the Catholic Church, none more popular than American Freedom and Catholic Power *(1949). Hundreds of thousands of copies were sold over the next decade. In the passage below, Blanshard summarizes his position against the Catholic Church in the United States.*

γ   γ   γ

Probably no phase of our life is in greater need of candid discussion than the relationship of the Roman Catholic Church to American institutions, and certainly no important factor in our life has been more consistently neglected by responsible writers. The Catholic issue is not an easy subject to discuss objectively because most Americans have automatically accepted their attitudes on the subject from their parents, and they do not want those attitudes disturbed. They are Catholic or they are not Catholic. If they are Catholic, they tend to view their own Church with favor, and its critics with suspicion. If they are not Catholic, they tend to reverse the process and view all distinctively Catholic policies with doubt. Amer-

---

*Quoted in Paul Blanshard, *American Freedom and Catholic Power* (Boston, 1949), pp. 1, 5. Used by permission of Paul Blanshard, Jr.

ican Catholics and American non-Catholics both tend to leave the discussion of religious differences to denominational bigots; and many Americans have never had an opportunity to hear a reasoned and temperate discussion of the place of Catholic power in our national life. . . .

I believe that every American—Catholic and non-Catholic—has a duty to speak on the Catholic question, because the issues involved go to the heart of our culture and our citizenship. Plain speaking on this question involves many risks of bitterness, misunderstanding and even fanaticism, but the risks of silence are even greater. Any critic of the policies of the Catholic hierarchy must steel himself to being called "anti-Catholic," because it is part of the hierarchy's strategy of defense to place that brand upon all its opponents; and any critic must also reconcile himself to being called an enemy of the Catholic people, because the hierarchy constantly identifies its clerical ambitions with the supposed wishes of its people.

It is important, therefore, to distinguish between the American Catholic people and their Roman-controlled priests. The Catholic people of the United States fight and die for the same concept of freedom as do other Americans; they believe in the same fundamental ideals of democracy. If they controlled their own Church, the Catholic problem would soon disappear because, in the atmosphere of American freedom, they would adjust their Church's policies to American realities.

Unfortunately, the Catholic people of the United States are not citizens but *subjects* in their own religious commonwealth. The secular as well as the religious policies of their Church are made in Rome by an organization that is alien in spirit and control. The American Catholic people themselves have no representatives of their own choosing either in their own local hierarchy or in the Roman high command; and they are compelled by the very nature of their Church's authoritarian structure to accept nonreligious as well as religious policies that have been imposed upon them from abroad.

It is for this reason that I am addressing Catholics fully as much as non-Catholics in this book. American freedom is *their* freedom, and any curtailment of that freedom by clerical power is an even more serious matter for them than it is for non-Catholics. I know that many Catholics are as deeply disturbed as I am about the social policies of their Church's rulers; and they are finding it increasingly difficult to reconcile their convictions as American democrats with the philosophy of their priests, their hierarchy and their Pope.

READING NO. 30

FULTON SHEEN EXPLAINS WHY "LIFE IS WORTH LIVING", 1953*

Certainly the most influential priest during the 1950s was Monsignor (later Bishop) Fulton J. Sheen. Like a number of young dynamic priests, Sheen used mass communication techniques to reach millions of Americans. His popularity as a speaker led to a prime-time television show opposite the comedy of Milton Berle. No one gave Sheen's "Life is Worth Living" much of a chance against Berle, but they were wrong. Sheen attracted millions of Americans to their sets each week and eventually forced Berle off the air. It seemed many Americans wanted more than entertainment; they also were seeking spiritual nourishment. Sheen was able to deliver hope and give direction to this postwar generation. In the passage below from the script of one of his television shows, Sheen describes why "Life is Worth Living."

γ   γ   γ

Is life worth living, or is it dull and monotonous? Life *is* monotonous if it is meaningless; it is *not* monotonous if it has a purpose.

The prospect of seeing the same program on television for a number of weeks is this problem in minor form. Will not repetition of the same format, the same personality, the same chalk, the same blackboard, and the same angel create monotony? Repetition does generally beget boredom. However, two beautiful compensations have been given a television audience to avoid such boredom: one is a dial, the other is a wrist. Put both together and all the forces of science and advertising vanish into nothingness.

*Quoted in Fulton J. Sheen, *Life is Worth Living* (New York, 1953), pp. 1, 2–3, 5, 7, 9. Copyright © 1953, 1954 by Mission Foundation Inc., Copyright renewed 1986 by the Estate of Fulton J. Sheen. Used by permission of Doubleday, Inc. and the Estate of Fulton J. Sheen.

Life is monotonous if it has no goal or purpose. When we do not know why we are here or where we are going, then life is full of frustrations and unhappiness. When there is no goal or over-all purpose, people generally concentrate on motion. Instead of working toward an ideal, they keep changing the ideal and calling it "progress." They do not know where they are going, but they are certainly "on their way." . . .

Some change their philosophy of life with every book they read: one book sells them on Freud, the next on Marx; materialists one year, idealists the next; cynics for another period, and liberals for still another. They have their quivers full of arrows, but no fixed target. As no game makes the hunter tired of the sport, so the want of destiny makes the mind bored with life.

Boredom can lead to revolution. A boy is given a BB gun. If the father gives him a target, for example, a bull's-eye on the side of a barn or an old tin can, the boy is happy to shoot at it, and use his gun as it ought to be used. As soon as the target is rejected or ignored or not given, generally he goes in for shooting anything, particularly school windows. The revolutionary spirit in the world today is born of such purposeless and meaningless existence. . . .

Thus far we have considered one alternative: Life does not seem worth living if it has no goal or purpose. On the other hand, life is thrilling if it has a destiny.

What we call the ultimate purpose of life is one beyond all immediate or proximate goals, such as a man wanting to become a farmer, or a woman wanting to become a nurse. The purpose that survives when these lesser goals have been achieved, is the ultimate goal. No one can have two final purposes in life any more than he can walk to the right and left at the same time. The final purpose is, therefore, unique—the grand powerhouse whence flows the current for all the particular tasks of living. . . .

Many think, when we say that man's ultimate happiness is union with God, that God is to be conceived as something extrinsic to man, as a kind of a pious "extra," or that He is related to us as a reward for a good life, or as a medal is related to study. A gold medal at the end of the school year is not intrinsically related to study. Many do excellent work in

school and get no medals. God and the happiness of Heaven
are not related to us that way. Rather God and Heaven are
related to one another as blooming to a rose, or as a peach to
a peach tree, or as an acorn to an oak, namely, as our intrinsic
perfection without which we are incomplete, and with which
we are happy. . . .

Because God is full of life, I imagine each morning Almighty God says to the sun, "Do it again"; and every evening
to the moon and the stars, "Do it again"; and every spring-
time to the daisies, "Do it again"; and every time a child is
born into the world asking for a curtain call, that the heart of
the God might once more ring out in the heart of the babe.

Life is full of romance and thrill when it has one over-all
purpose, namely, to be one with a Life that is Personal enough
to be a Father; one with a Truth that is Personal enough to be
the Wisdom from whence come all Art and Science; and one
that is Personal enough to be a Love that is a "Passionless
Passion, a wild Tranquility."

Life is Worth Living when we live each day to become
closer to God. When you have said your prayers, offered your
actions in union with God, continue to enjoy the "Thrill of
Monotony," and *Do it again!*

READING NO. 31

JOHN TRACY ELLIS ON AMERICAN CATHOLIC INTELLECTUAL LIFE, 1955*

Even though American Catholics had devoted considerable resources to the establishment of schools and colleges, the Church in the United States was almost devoid of an intellectual life. For more than a century, Catholic educational establishments had focused on two goals—preserving the religious faith of their students and preparing them for productive careers in American society. There was little encouragement of learning for learning's sake; indeed, those few Catholic intellectuals who spoke out with new or innovative ideas were criticized and isolated by their fellow Catholics. Father (later Monsignor) John Tracy Ellis detailed the poverty of American Catholic intellectual life in an address he presented in 1955. As a professor of history at the Catholic University of America and one of the leading scholars of American Catholicism, his comments could not be ignored. The address was discussed in dozens of journals and books at the time of publication, but little was done to remedy the state of Catholic intellectual life until the 1960s.

γ   γ   γ

In 1941 one of the most perceptive of living foreign observers of American life and institutions, Denis W. Brogan, professor of political science in the University of Cambridge, stated in a book on the United States: ". . . in no Western society is the intellectual prestige of Catholicism lower than in the country where, in such respects as wealth, numbers, and strength of organization, it is so powerful." No well-informed American Catholic will attempt to challenge that statement.

*Quoted in John Tracy Ellis, "American Catholics and the Intellectual Life," *Thought* 30 (Autumn, 1955): 353, 385–386. Reprinted by permission of the publisher, Fordham University Press. Copyright © 1955 by Fordham University Press.

Admittedly, the weakest aspect of the Church in this country lies in its failure to produce national leaders and to exercise commanding influence in intellectual circles, and this at a time when the number of Catholics in the United States is exceeded only by those of Brazil and Italy, and their material resources are incomparably superior to those of any other branch of the universal Church. What, one may ask, is the explanation of this striking discrepancy? . . . [American Catholics] have suffered from the timidity that characterizes minority groups, from the effects of a ghetto they have themselves fostered, and, too, from a sense of inferiority induced by their consciousness of the inadequacy of Catholic scholarship. But who, one may rightly ask, has been responsible in the main for its inadequacy? Certainly not the Church's enemies, for if one were to reason on that basis St. Augustine would never have written the *City of God,* St. Robert Bellarmine the *Tractatus de potestate summi pontificis,* nor would Cardinal Baronius have produced the *Annales ecclesiastici.* In fact, it has been enmity and opposition that have called forth some of the greatest monuments to Catholic scholarship. The major defect, therefore, lies elsewhere than with the unfriendly attitude of some of those outside the Church. The chief blame, I firmly believe, lies with Catholics themselves. It lies in their frequently self-imposed ghetto mentality which prevents them from mingling as they should with their non-Catholic colleagues, and in their lack of industry and the habits of work, to which [Robert] Hutchins alluded in 1937. It lies in their failure to have measured up to their responsibilities to the incomparable tradition of Catholic learning of which they are the direct heirs, a failure which Peter Viereck noted, and which suggested to him the caustic question, ''Is the honorable adjective 'Roman Catholic' truly merited by America's middle class-Jansenist Catholicism, puritanized, Calvinized, and dehydrated . . . ?'' When the inescapable and exacting labor of true scholarship is intelligently directed and competently expressed it will win its way on its own merits into channels of influence beyond the Catholic pale. Of that one can be certain. . . .

READING NO. 32

JOHN COURTNEY MURRAY ON CATHOLICISM AND DEMOCRACY, 1960*

Few scholars would dispute the claim that Father John Courtney Murray was the leading Catholic intellectual of his day. As editor of the prestigious journal Theological Studies *and as the author of numerous articles on church-state relations, Murray helped to shape the thinking of the generation of American bishops who would participate in the Second Vatican Council. During the early 1950s. Murray's views were considered controversial and he was forbidden by the Vatican to write on church-state relations. But by the end of the decade, the force of his ideas could no longer be suppressed and he was widely hailed in both the religious and the secular press. The 1960 publication of his book,* We Hold These Truths, *was something of a media event with* Time *magazine featuring Father Murray on the cover of one of its weekly issues. Murray's lasting contribution to American Catholicism, however, was the Declaration on Religious Liberty promulgated by the bishops at Vatican II. In the passage below from* We Hold These Truths, *Murray summarizes his ideas on the relationship between Catholicism and American democracy.*

γ   γ   γ

. . . The question is sometimes raised, whether Catholicism is compatible with American democracy. The question is invalid as well as impertinent; for the manner of its position inverts the order of values. It must, of course, be turned round to read, whether American democracy is compatible with Catholicism. The question, thus turned, is part of the civil question, as put to me. An affirmative answer to it, given under

*Quoted in John Courtney Murray, S.J., *We Hold These Truths: Catholic Reflections on the American Proposition* (New York, 1960), pp. ix–xii. Used by permission of Sheed & Ward, 115 E. Armour Blvd., Kansas City, MO.

something better than curbstone definition of "democracy,"
is one of the truths I hold.

The American Proposition makes a particular claim upon
the reflective attention of the Catholic in so far as it contains a
doctrine and a project in the matter of the "pluralist society,"
as we seem to have agreed to call it. The term might have
many meanings. By pluralism here I mean the coexistence
within the one political community of groups who hold divergent and incompatible views with regard to religious questions—those ultimate questions that concern the nature and
destiny of man within a universe that stands under the reign of
God. Pluralism therefore implies disagreement and dissension
within the community. But it also implies a community within
which there must be agreement and consensus. There is no
small political problem here. If society is to be at all a rational
process, some set of principles must motivate the general participation of all religious groups, despite their dissensions, in
the oneness of the community. On the other hand, these common principles must not hinder the maintenance by each group
of its own different identity. The problem of pluralism is, of
course, practical; as a project, its "working out" is an exercise in civic virtue. But the problem is also theoretical; its
solution is an exercise in political intelligence that will lay
down, as the basis for the "working out," some sort of doctrine.

As it found place in America the problem of pluralism was
unique in the modern world, chiefly because pluralism was
the native condition of American society. It was not, as in
Europe and in England, the result of the disruption and decay
of a previously existent religious unity. This fact made possible a new project; but the new project required, as its basis, a
new doctrine. This requirement was met by the First Amendment to the Constitution, in itself and in its relation to the
whole theory of limited government that the Constitution in-
corporates.

On any showing the First Amendment was a great act of
political intelligence. However, as in the case of all such acts,
precisely because they are great, the question arises, how this
act is to be understood. Concretely, what is the doctrine of the
First Amendment? How do you define the project that it

launched? On what grounds does the First Amendment command the common assent and consent of the whole citizenry? And how is it that this common assent and consent do not infringe upon the "freedom of religion," that is, the freedom of consciences to retain the full integrity of their own convictions, and the freedom of the churches to maintain their own different identities, as defined by themselves. I take it that every church claims this freedom to define itself, and claims too the consequent right to reject definition at the hands of any secular authority. To resign this freedom or to abdicate this right would be at once the betrayal of religion and the corruption of politics.

These questions, I presume, are put to every citizen, when he undertakes to articulate for himself the fundamental civil question, what are the truths we hold. They are put with special sharpness to the Catholic intelligence. Not that the questions themselves are embarrassing, but that the inner exigencies of the Catholic intelligence are high. The Catholic may not, as others do, merge his religious and his patriotic faith, or submerge one in the other. The simplist solution is not for him. He must reckon with his own tradition of thought, which is wider and deeper than any that America has elaborated. He must also reckon with his own history, which is longer than the brief centuries that America has lived. At the same time, he must recognize that a new problem has been put to the universal Church by the American doctrine and project in the matter of pluralism, as stated in the First Amendment. The conceptual equipment for dealing with the problem is by no means lacking to the Catholic intelligence. But there is the obligation of some nicety in its use, lest the new problem be distorted or the ancient faith deformed. . . .

There has, indeed, been considerable improvement among American Catholics in the realm of intellectual affairs in the last half-century, but the need for far more energetic strides is urgent if the receptive attitude of contemporary thought is to be capitalized upon as it should be. It is, therefore, a unique opportunity that lies before the Catholic scholars of the United States which, if approached and executed with the deep conviction of its vital importance for the future of the American Church, may inspire them to do great things and, at the end, to feel that they have in some small measure lived up to the ideal expressed by Pére Sertillanges when he said of the Catholic intellectuals:

> They, more than others, must be men consecrated by their vocation. . . . The special asceticism and the heroic virtue of the intellectual worker must be their daily portion. But if they consent to this double self-offering, I tell them in the name of God of Truth not to lose courage.

READING NO. 33

JOHN F. KENNEDY ON CATHOLICISM AND THE PRESIDENCY, 1960*

The question of whether or not a Catholic could serve as President of the United States had been raised first in the 1928 elections, but never satisfactorily answered. It was no surprise, therefore, that this question emerged once again when Senator John F. Kennedy announced his plans to run for President in 1960. The religion issue dogged Kennedy throughout the primaries and even after he had won the Democratic nomination. Learning from Al Smith's experience in 1928, Kennedy took the religious issue very seriously and constantly stressed his belief in the separation of church and state, his opposition to diplomatic relations with the Vatican, and his opposition to public aid to parochial schools. The religion issue came to a climax in September, 1960, with the formation of a national organization of ministers that opposed Kennedy for President because of his Catholicism. Kennedy responded to the group's concerns in an address to the Greater Houston Ministerial Association. It was a masterful speech that was given wide media coverage and it largely ended concerns about Kennedy's religion. The passage below is from that speech.

γ　　　　　γ　　　　　γ

. . . I believe in an America where the separation of church and state is absolute—where no Catholic prelate would tell the President (should he be a Catholic) how to act and no Protestant minister would tell his parishioners for whom to vote— where no church or church school is granted any public funds or political preference—and where no man is denied public office merely because his religion differs from the President who might appoint him or the people who might elect him.

I believe in an America that is officially neither Catholic,

*Quoted in *The New York Times*, September 13, 1960.

195

Protestant nor Jewish—where no public official either requests or accepts instructions on public policy from the Pope, the National Council of Churches or any other ecclesiastical source—where no religious body seeks to impose its will directly or indirectly upon the general populace or the public acts of its officials—and where religious liberty is so indivisible that an act against one church is treated as an act against all.

For, while this year it may be a Catholic against whom the finger of suspicion is pointed, in other years it has been, and may someday be again, a Jew—or a Quaker—or a Unitarian—or a Baptist. It was Virginia's harassment of Baptist preachers, for example, that led to Jefferson's statute of religious freedom. Today, I may be the victim—but tomorrow it may be you—until the whole fabric of our harmonious society is ripped apart at a time of great national peril.

Finally, I believe in an America where religious intolerance will someday end—where all men and all churches are treated as equal—where every man has the same right to attend or not to attend the church of his choice—where there is no Catholic vote, no anti-Catholic vote, no bloc voting of any kind—and where Catholics, Protestants and Jews, both the lay and the pastoral level, will refrain from those attitudes of disdain and division which have so often marred their works in the past, and promote instead the American ideal of brotherhood.

That is the kind of America in which I believe. And it represents the kind of Presidency in which I believe—a great office that must be neither humbled by making it the instrument of any religious group, nor tarnished by arbitrarily withholding it, its occupancy from the members of any religious group. I believe in a President whose views on religion are his own private affair, neither imposed upon him by the nation or imposed by the nation upon him as a condition to holding that office. . . .

But let me stress again that these are my views—for, contrary to common newspaper usage, I am not the Catholic candidate for President. I am the Democratic party's candidate for President who happens also to be a Catholic.

I do not speak for my church on public matters—and the church does not speak for me.

Whatever issue may come before me as President, if I should be elected—on birth control, divorce, censorship, gambling, or any other subject—I will make my decision in accordance with these views, in accordance with what my conscience tells me to be in the national interest, and without regard to outside religious pressure or dictate. And no power or threat of punishment could cause me to decide otherwise.

But if the time should ever come—and I do not concede any conflict to be remotely possible—when my office would require me to either violate my conscience, or violate the national interest, then I would resign the office, and I hope any other conscientious public servant would do likewise.

. . . I do not intend to apologize for these views to my critics of either Catholic or Protestant faith, nor do I intend to disavow either my views or my church in order to win this election. If I should lose on the real issues, I shall return to my seat in the Senate satisfied that I tried my best and was fairly judged.

But if this election is decided on the basis that 40,000,000 Americans lost their chance of being President on the day they were baptized, that it is the whole nation that will be the loser in the eyes of Catholics and non-Catholics around the world, in the eyes of history, and in the eyes of our own people.

But if, on the other hand, I should win this election, I shall devote every effort of mind and spirit to fulfilling the oath of the Presidency—practically identical, I might add, with the oath I have taken for fourteen years in the Congress. For, without reservation, I can, and I quote ''solemnly swear that I will faithfully execute the office of President of the United States and will to the best of my ability preserve, protect and defend the Constitution, so help me God.'' . . .

READING NO. 34

JOHN WRIGHT DEFENDS RELIGIOUS LIBERTY AT VATICAN II, 1964*

The impact of Vatican II on the lives of American Catholics has been extensive. Changes in Church attitudes on the liturgy, ecumenism, and the religious life touched virtually every American Catholic. One of the most important issues to the American Catholic bishops was religious liberty, a concept accepted by American Catholics for more than two centuries, but a principle not generally accepted within the Church. The American bishops fought hard for a declaration on religious liberty, arguing that a person's right to religious freedom was based on Catholic principles and a "pastoral necessity of the first order." In the end nearly 2,000 of the 2,200 bishops present at the session voted for the decree. It was an American triumph. The passage below is from the council commentary of Bishop (later Cardinal) John Wright, one of the leaders of the fight for the Declaration.

γ   γ   γ

. . . All sides agree that the question of religious liberty and its exercise ultimately touches the question of the common good. Therefore, the analysis and defense of religious liberty ought to take into account the nature and protection of that common good which, in a way, constitutes the very *res publica* and thus must be promoted by the directors of the State.

There are those who strongly assert that the defense of religious liberty, even for those who set forth errors contrary to Catholic truth, disrupts or damages the common good, which indeed can scarcely be denied at times. On the contrary, there are those who affirm, from another angle, that paradoxical though it be, the denial of recognition to religious liberty, in its own way and often to a far worse degree, harms the com-

---

*Quoted in Vincent Yzermans, ed., *American Participation in the Second Vatican Council* (New York, 1967), pp. 653, 655–656.

198

mon good, because the common good by its very nature positively demands and presumes as an integral and essential element such liberty and its recognition by the civil power. It is on this point that I have a few things I should like to say. . . .

Those who seek the common good in its full and true sense—and according to authentic Catholic teaching with the philosophical and theological principles to which our *practice* ought to conform and not *vice versa*—those who defend such a common good will wish to strengthen, foster and extend as far as possible all truly human liberties, especially religious liberty, that is, the liberty to learn, to meditate and to worship the Supreme Good, God, the source and author of all goods. Such religious liberty can be worked out even in a State favoring some particular religion for historical reasons—as it does in England, where a Protestant Church (the so-called Established Church) traditionally enjoys special privileges, but where now, at least, all, except the King and Queen (unless I am mistaken), have full religious liberty. The case of Ireland is also pertinent, for there the Catholic Church is held in special esteem by the Constitution and in certain customs, but all enjoy full religious liberty. As a matter of fact—and it should be acknowledged openly—religious liberty is often more complete in other countries than it is in America; this is certainly the case in England with regard to school rights, and it also is so in Holland.

There can be no doubt that Catholics—and especially the pastors of souls—will pray and work tirelessly to the end that all men will use their liberty to advance to the full and perfect knowledge of the one true God and Him whom God sent, Jesus Christ. We will be witnesses to Him to the very ends of the earth, witnesses by word and deed. We will debate, we will implore, we will rebuke in all patience and in the light of true doctrine, so that error may have no *place,* whether or not it has any *right;* but we shall do this always recognizing the rights of any who are in error. *We* will fulfill our right and duty with the help of the grace of Christ, in the light of the Gospel, by the power of the Holy Spirit and armed with the spiritual might of the Church, neither fearing nor exploiting the constraining power of the kingdoms of this world. Whatever may be said of times past and of political cultures once, perhaps, more consistent with the work of the Gospel, but now obsolete, it is now, in the present order, necessary that Christians ask of the civil power only that it respect in justice our right to fulfill the commands of Christ; that it assist in justice our efforts to play our rightful and necessary part in furthering the common good through our work in behalf of education and peace; and that it leave inviolate, as a matter of justice, the religious liberty of all those for whom the message of the Gospels and the grace of Christ are destined, namely *all men*.

God, who gave us the duty, right and liberty to preach, gave those to whom we preach the duty, right and liberty of hearing and believing as a means to that religious perfection which the civil power can neither give nor take away, and which, therefore, it should scrupulously respect, especially as regards its liberty.

We, the successors of the Apostles, men of God, bishops of the Catholic Church—we ought to be foremost and fearless leaders among the heralds of liberty, because historically we are the heirs of liberty in matters religious acquired almost in every case and almost in every nation only through the blood and tears of our fathers. Thus we know from the experience of our own history how dear and how fruitful liberty is. Much more, supernaturally we are heirs of an even greater liberty, the liberty by which Christ has made us free by His own free obedience—a free obedience which we will freely imitate, always in the hope and with the purpose of freely persuading our neighbors and brothers to a similar free obedience—a liberty that is saving because it is obedient, an obedience that saves because it is free.

READING NO. 35

CHARLES CURRAN ON CONTRACEPTION AND SIN, 1966*

Vatican II set off a change in American Catholic attitudes on controversial subjects such as birth control and divorce. The Council seemed to free Catholics from the bonds of guilt. Before Vatican II, lay Catholics generally followed the lead of their pastors on all spiritual and moral matters. After Vatican II, however, Catholics felt free to question the pronouncements of their priests, their bishops, and even the Pope. This lay Catholic independence was documented dramatically in the wide spread criticism of Pope Paul VI's encyclical Humanae Vitae *calling for an end to use of artificial contraception.*

Caught in the maelstrom of this change were a number of moral theologians who defended the right of lay Catholics to make their own decisions on these matters. In the passage below, Father Charles Curran of the Catholic University of America, describes how he came to his views on contraception and sin.

γ   γ   γ

. . . Contact and dialogue with many married Christians forced me to reconsider my views. Many couples found themselves in the dilemma of realizing a need to express their love in a human way and yet dared not have any more children. Family love and marriages were weakened and at times almost destroyed because couples could not fully express their love in a sexual way. The question arose almost instinctively—would such a couple be breaking their relationship with God by using contraception? In some cases I was sure that the couple would not be guilty of mortal sin.

*Quoted in Charles E. Curran, *Christian Morality Today* (Notre Dame, 1966), pp. 68–69, 76. Used by permission of the author.

Some had taken the risk and decided to use contraception. Many other conscientious non-Catholic Christians are doing the same. Are they breaking their relationship with God? How can I tell? The criterion frequently proposed in scripture is the love of our neighbor. How can we love the God we do not see if we cannot love our neighbor whom we do see? The last judgment as portrayed in Matthew's account bases man's relationship with God on his relationship with his fellow men. "For when I was hungry, you gave me food; when thirsty, you gave me drink. . . ." (Matt 25:31–46). Some people using contraception are most generous in their love of God and neighbor. A good number have followed the teaching of the Church, but now find that their marriage, their health, and their finances persuade them not to have any more children. They are devoted husbands and wives, fathers and mothers; they give of their few moments of free time in projects for the betterment of society; they are kind to all; they go out of their way to help others; they try to overcome their feelings of vengeance and rancor. By their fruits you will know them. They seem to be good Christians who have not broken their relationship with God.

Theologians have always admitted that something can be objectively sinful even though for a particular person because of subjective circumstances it might not be a subjective sin. But the frequency of the subjective occurrence does raise doubts about the objective sinfulness. . . .

However, it could be that in a particular case for a particular couple in their individual circumstances the use of contraceptives might not break their relationship with God. Theologians have always admitted that in certain circumstances there might not be subjective guilt. Chancery officials today frequently imply that suicides are not guilty of grave sin. No confessor believes that all acts of masturbation confessed by adolescents are subjectively serious sins. A couple might come to the conclusion that in their particular circumstances contraception is needed to preserve very important values in their lives.

The ultimate judgment must always be made by the individual couple. I try to see from their whole life if they have broken their relationship with God. I apply the criteria mentioned in first part of the essay with regard to their relationships with one another, with their family, their fellow workers, their neighbors, and their enemies. The fact they have made a real effort in the past would argue for their good faith. I encourage them to continue building up their relationship with God and each other. The decision to use contraception is difficult and risky. The danger of self-deception is ever present, but there are times when contraception might be necessary for an individual couple. I have counselled couples along these lines.

READING NO. 36

THE "CATONSVILLE NINE" ON THE VIETNAM WAR, 1968*

The 1960s were a decade of social action and reform within the Catholic Church in the United States. The civil rights movement, Vatican II, the Vietnam war, and other events during these years encouraged and compelled American Catholics to make their feelings known through protest. Among the most active and visible Catholic protesters were two brothers, Daniel and Philip Berrigan. Both brothers were ordained priests who had been active in the social justice causes of the 1950s. But the Berrigans were best known for their 1960s protests against the immorality of the war in Vietnam, particularly for their 1968 break-in at a U.S. Selective Service office in Catonsville, Maryland. With seven other protesters, the Berrigans used homemade napalm (a defoliant used in the Vietnam war) to burn U.S. Selective Service files. For this crime, the "Catonsville Nine" were tried, convicted, and given prison sentences, but the Berrigans succeeded in conveying their message. By 1972, most Americans were weary of the war and eager for U.S. troops to return home. Below is the statement of the Catonsville Nine at the time of their arrest.

γ γ γ

. . . Above all, our protest attempts to illustrate why our country is torn at home and harassed abroad by enemies of its own creation. For a long time the United States has been an empire, and today it is history's richest nation. Representing 6 per cent of the world's people, our country controls half the world's productive capacity and two-thirds of its finance. It holds Northern and Southern America in an economic vise. In fifteen years time, economists think that its industry in Europe

*Quoted in Philip Berrigan, *A Punishment for Peace* (New York, 1969), pp. 171–174. Reprinted with permission of Macmillan Publishing Company. Copyright © 1969 by Philip Berrigan, S.S.J.

will be the third greatest industrial power in the world, after the United States and the Soviet Union. Our foreign profits run substantially higher than domestic profits. So industry flees abroad under Government patronage and protection from the CIA, counter-insurgency, and conflict management teams.

The military participates with economic and political sectors to form a triumvirate of power which sets and enforces policy. With an annual budget of more than 80 billion dollars, our military now controls over half of all Federal property (53 per cent, or 183 billion dollars) while U.S. nuclear and conventional weaponry exceeds that of the whole remaining world. . . .

We believe that some property has no right to exist. Hitler's gas ovens, Stalin's concentration camps, atomic-bacteriological-chemical weaponry, files of conscription, and slum properties have no right to exist. When people starve for bread and lack decent housing, it is usually because the rich debase themselves with abuse of property, causing extravagance on their part and oppression and misery in others. . . .

We confront the Catholic Church, other Christian bodies, and the synagogues of America with their silence and cowardice in the face of our country's crimes. We are convinced that the religious bureaucracy in this country is racist, guilty of complicity in war, and hostile to the poor. In utter fidelity to our faith, we indict religious leaders and their followers for their failure to serve our country and mankind.

Finally, we are appalled by the ruse of the American ruling class invoking pleas for "law and order" to mask and perpetuate injustice. Let our President and the pillars of society speak of "law and justice" and back up their words with deeds. Then there will be "order." We have pleaded, spoken, marched, and nursed the victims of their injustice. Now this injustice must be faced, and this we intend to do, with whatever strength of mind, body, and grace that God will give us. May He have mercy on our nation.

Rev. Daniel Berrigan	Majorie Bradford Melville
Rev. Philip Berrigan	Thomas Melville
Bro. David Darst	George Mische
John Hogan	Mary Moylan
Thomas Lewis	

READING NO. 37

ANDREW GREELEY ON THE DECLINE OF CATHOLIC EDUCATION, 1976*

Vatican II had a significant impact on parochial education in the United States. The council had precipitated an identity crisis among many of the women religious who staffed parochial classrooms and it also caused Catholic parents to question the value and the purpose of Catholic schools. The doubts about parochial education were manifest in the steady decline in enrollments and the rise in the number of school closings. During the two decades following Vatican II, twenty-seven percent of the Catholic parochial schools and forty percent of the Catholic high schools in the United States closed their doors for good. Enrollments had risen 142 percent in the years from 1945 to 1962, but each year after 1965 saw a marked decrease in the number. Total enrollment dropped from a high of 5.6 million students in 1965 to less than 3 million by the mid-1980s.

There has been no more knowledgeable and controversial an authority on the nature and decline of American Catholic parochial education than Father Andrew Greeley, a University of Chicago-trained sociologist who has written widely on the topic. The passage below is from a major sociological study he wrote in the midst of the crisis.

γ   γ   γ

Timid, cautious administrators that they are (with such marvelous blunders on the record as the two million dollars invested in Penn Central paper shortly before that railroad went bankrupt), the American Catholic hierarchy has been appalled at the skyrocketing costs of parochial education. It is apparently un-

---

*Quoted in Andrew M. Greeley, William C. McCready, and Kathleen McCourt, *Catholic Schools in a Declining Church* (Kansas City, 1976), pp. 324–326. Used by permission of the author.

aware of the dramatic increase in the Catholic standard of living that has occurred in the last quarter of a century. (Real income between 1945 and 1975 has more than doubled for American Catholics.) Catholics have far more ''disposable income'' to spend on parochial schools now than they did in the 1930s, and there is every reason to think that they are ready to dispose of substantially more of that income in support of Catholic schools than they were in the past. Changes in the administration and financing of Catholic education would be absolutely imperative to making such funds available, but there is so much caution and fear and mediocrity in the leadership of the American church that it seems much easier to close schools down or to refuse to build new ones than to risk innovative techniques of administering and funding Catholic schools. While the hierarchy is not usually sensitive to the party line of the liberal-left Catholic intelligentsia, the opposition of this group to the schools has provided the hierarchy with a convenient rationale for phasing out Catholic education—all the while, of course, pretending to endorse it enthusiastically.

Quite bluntly, the hierarchy should get out of the Catholic education business and turn the funding and administration of the schools over to the laity. There is, of course, great fear expressed at such a suggestion. How could the laity handle such a task? (As though there was not a nation across our borders to the north where the laity have more than adequately demonstrated that they could.) If Catholic parents want parochial schools, then they should be responsible for the funding and administration of them. If they cannot raise the money for the schools within the Catholic population (and our data suggests that they can), then it is they and not the hierarchy who should organize a campaign to force the Supreme Court to reverse its bigoted decisions on the subject of Catholic schools. To proceed on such a path would involve a substantial surrender of power, of course, by the bishops and by the parish clergy. No one likes to surrender power; no one likes to think of money, especially ''Catholic money,'' being spent without having much say about how it is spent. What is the point of being a bishop, after all, if you don't have the ultimate power of the purse strings? Why be a bishop at all if other people are responsible for spending *your* money?

Nor does it appear that the Catholic intelligentsia has ever really stopped to consider that Catholic schools are not an inkblot onto which one can project one's aggressions and frustrations toward the institutional church. It also seems not to have occurred to them that at a time when alternative education is becoming a very important issue among America's secular intelligentsia, the only large and functioning alternative to the moribund state educational monopoly is the Catholic schools. The hundreds and thousands of black parents who are sending their children to Catholic schools in the inner city know what is the available alternative to the monstrously inept public school bureaucratic monopoly. But the Catholic intelligentsia is so interested in outnativing the nativists that it has been thus far afraid to seriously explore the contribution and to defend the existence of an alternative religious education system. Indeed, all one has to do is to say something positive about Catholic schools in Official Liberal Catholic quarters and one is immediately deemed a conservative. At one time, one's badge of Official Liberalism was the proud announcement that one had pulled one's children out of the parochial schools. It is interesting to note that at least some people have had sense enough to change their minds and have since put their children back into the schools. When *Commonweal* carries an article entitled, ''Why I Sent My Children Back to Catholic Schools,'' we will know that the Catholic intelligentsia has turned the corner.

Just as *Humanae Vitae* was more the result of a system failure than of individual malice, so the bizarre paradox of Catholic schools in the United States is a result of system failure. Attendance declines and construction comes to a halt because those in decision-making positions are unaware of the support for and the importance of Catholic schools for the overwhelming majority of American Catholics. American Catholicism is not structured in such a way that the attitudes of the laity are communicated upward or that periodic evaluation of institutional effectiveness can occur. The hierarchy and the intelligentsia may disagree on many things, but they agree on one thing: their minds are made up—they need not be bothered by evidence of what ordinary people think or of how effective the various institutional apostolates of the church might be. The ordinary lay person takes for granted that nobody cares much what he thinks. And most laity are inclined to accept passively decisions that are made by ecclesiastical leadership and to ignore the advice and conventional wisdom offered by the intelligentsia.

Catholic schools, an extraordinarily powerful asset of the American church, will go down the drain with hardly a voice raised in protest because the decision-making system of the American church has permitted a policy to evolve concerning the schools which virtually guarantees their continued decline. It is again not a question of malice but of systematic ignorance, that is to say, ignorance built into the decision-making system.

READING NO. 38

THE CATHOLIC BISHOPS ON THE CHALLENGE OF PEACE, 1983*

One of the most powerful and controversial pastoral statements issued by the American Catholic bishops in recent years has been The Challenge of Peace: God's Promise and Our Response. *Issued on May 3, 1983, the statement included a strong and forceful call for bilateral nuclear disarmament. Such a call, coming as it did in the midst of the Reagan administration's efforts to increase the defense budget and fund the "Strategic Defense Initiative," was both praised and criticized as a political statement. The bishops stood their ground: "The whole world must summon the moral courage and the technical means to say 'no' to nuclear conflict; 'no' to weapons of mass destruction; 'no' to an arms race which robs the poor and the vulnerable; and 'no' to the moral danger of a nuclear age which places before human-kind indefensible choices of constant terror and surrender. Peace-making is not an optional commitment. It is a requirement of our faith."*

γ   γ   γ

PEACE IN THE MODERN WORLD: RELIGIOUS PERSPECTIVES AND PRINCIPLES

. . . 5. The global threat of nuclear war is a central concern of the universal Church, as the words and deeds of recent popes and the Second Vatican Council vividly demonstrate. In this pastoral letter we speak as bishops of the universal Church, heirs of the religious and moral teaching on modern warfare of the last four decades. We also speak as bishops of the Church in the United States, who have both the obligation

---

*Quoted in Hugh J. Nolan, ed., *Pastoral Letters of the U.S. Catholic Bishops* (Washington, 1984), vol. 4, pp. 494–499. Used by permission of the U.S. Catholic Conference.

and the opportunity to share and interpret the moral and religious wisdom of the Catholic tradition by applying it to the problems of war and peace today.

6. The nuclear threat transcends religious, cultural, and national boundaries. To confront its danger requires all the resources reason and faith can muster. This letter is a contribution to a wider common effort, meant to call Catholics and all members of our political community to dialogue and specific decisions about this awesome question.

7. The Catholic tradition on war and peace is a long and complex one, reaching from the Sermon on the Mount to the statements of Pope John Paul II. Its development cannot be sketched in a straight line and it seldom gives a simple answer to complex questions. It speaks through many voices and has produced multiple forms of religious witness. As we locate ourselves in this tradition, seeking to draw from it and develop it, the document which provides profound inspiration and guidance for us is the *Pastoral Constitution on the Church in the Modern World* of Vatican II, for it is based on doctrinal principles and addresses the relationship of the Church to the world with respect to the most urgent issues of our day. . . .

13. The *Pastoral Constitution* calls us to bring the light of the Gospel to bear upon "the signs of the times." Three signs of the times have particularly influenced the writing of this letter. The first, to quote Pope John Paul II at the United Nations, is that "the world wants peace, the world needs peace." The second is the judgment of Vatican II about the arms race: "The arms race is one of the greatest curses on the human race and the harm it inflicts upon the poor is more than can be endured." The third is the way in which the unique dangers and dynamics of the nuclear arms race present qualitatively new problems which must be addressed by fresh applications of traditional moral principles. In light of these three characteristics, we wish to examine Catholic teaching on peace and war. . . .

16. Catholic teaching on peace and war has had two purposes: to help Catholics form their consciences and to contribute to the public policy debate about the morality of war. These two purposes have led Catholic teaching to address two distinct but overlapping audiences. The first is the Catholic

faithful, formed by the premises of the Gospel and the principles of Catholic moral teaching. The second is the wider civil
community, a more pluralistic audience, in which our brothers
and sisters with whom we share the name Christian, Jews,
Moslems, other religious communities, and all people of good
will also make up our polity. Since Catholic teaching has traditionally sought to address both audiences, we intend to
speak to both in this letter, recognizing that Catholics are also
members of the wider political community.

17. The conviction, rooted in Catholic ecclesiology, that
both the community of the faithful and the civil community
should be addressed on peace and war has produced two complementary but distinct styles of teaching. The religious community shares a specific perspective of faith and can be called
to live out its implications. The wider civil community, although it does not share the same vision of faith, is equally
bound by certain key moral principles. For all men and
women find in the depth of their consciences a law written on
the human heart by God. From this law reason draws moral
norms. These norms do not exhaust the Gospel vision, but
they speak to critical questions affecting the welfare of the
human community, the role of states in international relations,
and the limits of acceptable action by individuals and nations
on issues of war and peace. . . .

21. Building peace within and among nations is the work of
many individuals and institutions; it is the fruit of ideas and
decisions taken in the political, cultural, economic, social,
military, and legal sectors of life. We believe that the Church,
as a community of faith and social institution, has a proper,
necessary, and distinctive part to play in the pursuit of peace.

22. The distinctive contribution of the Church flows from
her religious nature and ministry. The Church is called to be,
in a unique way, the instrument of the Kingdom of God in
history. Since peace is one of the signs of that Kingdom
present in the world, the Church fulfills part of her essential
mission by making the peace of the Kingdom more visible in
our time.

23. Because peace, like the Kingdom of God itself, is both
a divine gift and a human work, the Church should continually
pray for the gift and share in the work. We are called to be a

Church at the service of peace, precisely because peace is one manifestation of God's word and work in our midst. Recognition of the Church's responsibility to join with others in the work of peace is a major force behind the call today to develop a theology of peace. Much of the history of Catholic theology on war and peace has focused on limiting the resort to force in human affairs; this task is still necessary, and is reflected later in this Pastoral Letter, but it is not a sufficient response to Vatican II's challenge ''to undertake a completely fresh reappraisal of war.''

24. A fresh reappraisal which includes a developed theology of peace will require contributions from several sectors of the Church's life: biblical studies, systematic and moral theology, ecclesiology, and the experience and insights of members of the Church who have struggled in various ways to make and keep the peace in this often violent age. This Pastoral Letter is more an invitation to continue the new appraisal of war and peace than a final synthesis of the results of such an appraisal. We have some sense of the characteristics of a theology of peace, but not a systematic statement of their relationships.

25. A theology of peace should ground the task of peacemaking solidly in the biblical vision of the Kingdom of God, then place it centrally in the ministry of the Church. It should specify the obstacles in the way of peace, as these are understood theologically and in the social and political sciences. It should both identify the specific contributions a community of faith can make to the work of peace and relate these to the wider work of peace pursued by other groups and institutions in society. Finally, a theology of peace must include a message of hope. The vision of hope must be available to all, but one source of its content should be found in a Church at the service of peace. . . .

READING NO. 39

JOSEPH BERNARDIN ON THE CONSISTENT ETHIC OF LIFE, 1984*

Cardinal Joseph Bernardin of Chicago was one of the principal authors of the Catholic bishops' 1983 pastoral statement on the challenge of peace. Yet Bernardin saw nuclear disarmament as only one aspect of what he called a "consistent ethic of life." Such an ethic challenged Catholics and other Christians to oppose all forms of human violence—capital punishment, genetic experimentation, euthanasia, and abortion, as well as modern warfare. Bernardin saw these issues as a "seamless garment"—that it was inconsistent for Christians to pick and choose among these issues, that Christians must be against all actions that threaten human life. As might be expected, Bernardin's views were considered controversial. Conservatives who agreed with the cardinal on abortion opposed him on capital punishment and nuclear disarmament. Liberals applauded Bernardin on nuclear disarmament and capital punishment, but opposed him on abortion. For many Catholics and Christians, however, Bernardin offered a framework for their pro-life activities. The passage below is from a speech he gave at Fordham University in New York.

γ   γ   γ

. . . The dominant cultural fact, present in both modern warfare and modern medicine, which induces a sharper awareness of the fragility of human life is our technology. To live as we do in an age of careening development of technology is to face a qualitative new range of moral problems. War has been a perennial threat to human life, but today the threat is qualitatively different due to nuclear weapons. We now threaten

* Quoted in Joseph Cardinal Bernardin, "A Consistent Ethic of Life: An American Catholic Dialogue, *Thought*, 59 (March 1984): 102–107. Reprinted by permission of the publisher, Fordham University Press. Copyright © 1984 by Fordham University Press.

life on a scale previously unimaginable. As the pastoral letter put it, the dangers of nuclear war teach us to read the Book of Genesis with new eyes. From the inception of life to its decline, a rapidly expanding technology opens new opportunities for care but also poses new potential to threaten the sanctity of life.

The technological challenge is a pervasive concern of Pope John Paul II, expressed in his first encyclical, *Redemptor Hominis,* and continuing through his address to the Pontifical Academy of Science last month when he called scientists to direct their work toward the promotion of life, not the creation of instruments of death. The essential question in the technological challenge is this: In an age when we *can* do almost anything, how do we decide what we *ought* to do? The even more demanding question is: In a time when we can do anything technologically, how do we decide morally what *we never should do?*

Asking these questions along the spectrum of life from womb to tomb creates the need for a consistent ethic of life. For the spectrum of life cuts across the issues of genetics, abortion, capital punishment, modern warfare, and the care of the terminally ill. These are all distinct problems, enormously complicated, and deserving individual treatment. No single answer and no simple responses will solve them. My purpose, however, is to highlight the way in which we face new technological challenges in each one of these areas; this combination of challenges is what cries out for a consistent ethic of life.

Such an ethic will have to be finely honed and carefully structured on the basis of values, principles, rules, and applications to specific cases. It is not my task today, nor within my competence as a bishop, to spell out all the details of such an ethic. It is to that task that philosophers and poets, theologians and technicians, scientists and strategists, political leaders and plain citizens are called. I would, however, highlight a basic issue: the need for an attitude or atmosphere in society which is the precondition for sustaining a consistent ethic of life. The development of such an atmosphere has been the primary concern of the ''Respect Life'' program of the American bishops. We intend our opposition to abortion and our opposition to nuclear war to be seen as specific applications of this broader attitude. We have also opposed the death penalty because we do not think its use cultivates an attitude of respect for life in society. The purpose of proposing a consistent ethic of life is to argue that success on any one of the issues threatening life requires a concern for the broader attitude in society about respect for human life.

The use of this principle exemplifies the meaning of a consistent ethic of life. The principle which structures both cases, war and abortion, needs to be upheld in both places. It cannot be successfully sustained on one count and simultaneously eroded in a similar situation. When one carries this principle into the public debate today, however, one meets significant opposition from very different places on the political and ideological spectrum. Some see clearly the application of the principle to abortion but contend the bishops overstepped their bounds when they applied it to choices about national security. Others understand the power of the principle in the strategic debate, but find its application on abortion a violation of the realm of private choice. I contend the viability of the principle depends upon the consistency of its application.

A consistent ethic of life must be held by a constituency to be effective. The building of such a constituency is precisely the task before the Church and the nation. There are two distinct challenges, but they are complementary.

We should begin with the honest recognition that the shaping of a consensus among Catholics in the spectrum of life issues is far from finished. We need the kind of dialogue on these issues which the pastoral letter generated on the nuclear question. We need the same searching intellectual exchange, the same degree of involvement of clergy, religious and laity, the same sustained attention in the Catholic press.

There is no better place to begin than by using the followthrough for the pastoral letter. Reversing the arms race, avoiding nuclear war and moving toward a world freed of the nuclear threat are profoundly ''pro-life'' issues. The Catholic Church is today seen as an institution and a community committed to these tasks. We should not lose this momentum; it provides a solid foundation to relate our concerns about war and peace to other ''pro-life'' questions. The agenda facing us involves our ideas and our institutions; it must be both educational and political; it requires attention to the way these several life issues are defined in the public debate and how they are decided in the policy process.

The shaping of a consensus in the Church must be joined to the larger task of sharing our vision with the wider society. Here two questions face us: the substance of our position and the style of our presence in the policy debate.

The substance of a Catholic position on a consistent ethic of life is rooted in a religious vision. But the citizenry of the United States is radically pluralistic in moral and religious conviction. So we face the challenge of stating our case, which is shaped in terms of our faith and our religious convictions, in nonreligious terms which others of different faith convictions might find morally persuasive. Here again the war and peace debate should be a useful model. We have found support from individuals and groups who do not share our Catholic faith but who have found our moral analysis compelling.

In the public policy exchange, substance and style are closely related. The issues of war, abortion, and capital punishment are emotional and often divisive questions. As we seek to shape and share the vision of a consistent ethic of life, I suggest a style governed by the following rule: We should maintain and clearly articulate our religious convictions but also maintain our civil courtesy. We should be vigorous in stating a case and attentive in hearing another's case; we should test everyone's logic but not question his or her motives.

The proposal I have outlined today is a multidimensional challenge. It grows out of the experience I have had in the war and peace debate and the task I see ahead as Chairman of the Pro-Life Committee. But it also grows from a conviction that there is a new openness today in society to the role of moral argument and moral vision in our public affairs. I say this even though I find major aspects of our domestic and foreign policy in need of drastic change. Bringing about these changes is the challenge of a consistent ethic of life. The challenge is worth our energy, resources, and commitment as a Church.

READING NO. 40

MARIO CUOMO ON RELIGIOUS BELIEF AND PUBLIC MORALITY, 1984*

Catholic political leaders have faced difficult issues in the 1980s, issues that put these men and women between the stand taken by their Church and the will of the people. There has been no more controversial issue during these years than abortion. Since the landmark Supreme Court decision in Roe v. Wade *in 1973, women in the United States have had the constitutional right to an abortion during the first months of pregnancy. The Catholic Church has vigorously condemned abortion in all instances and continues to work to overturn the Supreme Court decision. Thus, many Catholics who hold public office find themselves caught between upholding the law of the land or accepting the position of their Church.*

One of the most thoughtful discussions of this dilemma was presented by Governor Mario Cuomo of New York in a 1984 speech at the University of Notre Dame.

γ   γ   γ

. . . The Catholic Church is my spiritual home. My heart is there, and my hope.

There is, of course, more to being a Catholic than a sense of spiritual and emotional resonance. Catholicism is a religion of the head as well as the heart, and to be a Catholic is to say "I believe" to the essential core of dogmas that distinguishes our faith.

The acceptance of this faith requires a lifelong struggle to understand it more fully and to live it more truly, to translate truth into experience, to practice as well as to believe. . . .

I believe I have a salvific mission as a Catholic. Does that mean I am in conscience required to do everything I can as Governor to translate all my religious values into the laws and

*Quoted in *Law Studies,* 10 (April/May, 1985): 4–10.

regulations of the State of New York or the United States? Or be branded a hypocrite if I don't?

As a Catholic, I respect the teaching authority of the bishops.

But must I agree with everything in the bishops' pastoral letter on peace and fight to include it in party platforms?

And will I have to do the same for the forthcoming pastoral on economics even if I am an unrepentant supply sider?

Must I, having heard the Pope renew the Church's ban on birth control devices, veto the funding of contraceptive programs for non-Catholics or dissenting Catholics in my State?

I accept the Church's teaching on abortion. Must I insist you do? By law? By denying you Medicaid funding? By a constitutional amendment? If so, which one? Would that be the best way to avoid abortions or to prevent them?

These are only some of the questions for Catholics. People with other religious beliefs face similar problems.

Let me try some answers. . . .

As a Catholic, I have accepted certain answers as the right ones for myself and my family, and because I have, they have influenced me in special ways, as Matilda's husband, as a father of five children, as a son who stood next to his own father's death bed trying to decide if the tubes and needles no longer served a purpose.

As a Governor, however, I am involved in defining policies that determine other people's rights in these same areas of life and death. Abortion is one of these issues, and while it is one issue among many, it is one of the most controversial and affects me in a special way as a Catholic public official.

As Catholics, my wife and I were enjoined never to use abortion to destroy the life we created, and we never have. We thought Church doctrine was clear on this, and—more than that—both of us felt it in full agreement with what our hearts and our consciences told us. For me life or fetal life in the womb should be protected, even if five of nine Justices of the Supreme Court and my neighbor disagree with me. A fetus is different from an appendix or a set of tonsils. At the very least, even if the argument is made by some scientists or some theologians that in the early stages of fetal development we can't discern human life, the full potential of human life is indisputably there. That—to my less subtle mind—by itself should demand respect, caution, indeed . . . reverence.

But not everyone in our society agrees with me and Matilda.

And those who don't—those who endorse legalized abortions—aren't a ruthless, callous alliance of anti-Christians determined to overthrow our moral standards. In many cases, the proponents of legal abortion are the very people who have worked with Catholics to realize the goals of social justice set out in papal encyclicals: the American Lutheran Church, the Central Conference of American Rabbis, the Presbyterian Church in the United States, B'nai B'rith Women, the women of the Episcopal Church. These are just a few of the religious organizations that don't share the Church's position on abortion. . . .

Respectfully, and after careful consideration of the position and arguments of the bishops, I have concluded that the approach of a constitutional amendment is not the best way for us to seek to deal with abortion.

I believe that legal interdicting of abortion by either the federal government or the individual states is not a plausible possibility and even if it could be obtained, it wouldn't work. Given present attitudes, it would be "Prohibition" revisited, legislating what couldn't be enforced and in the process creating a disrespect for law in general. And as much as I admire the bishop's hope that a constitutional amendment against abortion would be the basis for a full, new bill of rights for mothers and children, I disagree that this would be the result. . . .

The hard truth is that abortion isn't a failure of government. No agency or department of government forces women to have abortions, but abortion goes on. Catholics, the statistics show, support the right to abortion in equal proportion to the rest of the population. Despite the teaching in our homes and schools and pulpits, despite the sermons and pleadings of parents and priests and prelates, despite all the effort at defining our opposition to the sin of abortion, collectively we Catholics apparently believe—and perhaps act—little differently from those who don't share our commitment.

We are asking government to make criminal what we believe to be sinful because we ourselves can't stop committing the sin?

The failure here is not Caesar's. The failure is our failure, the failure of the entire people of God. . . .

We cannot justify our aspiration to goodness simply on the basis of the vigor of our demand for an exclusive and questionable civil law declaring what we already know, that abortion is wrong.

Approval or rejection of legal restrictions on abortion should not be the exclusive litmus test of Catholic loyalty. We should understand that whether abortion is outlawed or not, our work has barely begun: the work of creating a society where the right to life doesn't end at the moment of birth; where an infant isn't helped into a world that doesn't care if it's fed properly, housed decently, educated adequately; where the blind or retarded child isn't condemned to exist rather than empowered to live. . . .

We Catholic citizens of the richest, most powerful nation that has ever existed are like the stewards made responsible over a great household: from those to whom so much has been given, much shall be required. It is worth repeating that ours is not a faith that encourages its believers to stand apart from the world, seeking their salvation alone, separate from the salvation of those around them.

We speak of ourselves as a body. We come together in worship as companions in the ancient sense of that word, those who break bread together, and who are obliged by the commitment we share to help one another, everywhere, in all we do, and in the process, to help the whole human family. We see our mission to be "the completion of the work of creation." . . .

We can be fully Catholic; proudly, totally at ease with ourselves, a people in the world, transforming it, a light to this nation. Appealing to the best in our people not the worst. Persuading not coercing. Leading people to truth by love. And still, all the while, respecting and enjoying our unique pluralistic democracy. And we can do it even as politicians.

READING NO. 41

THE CATHOLIC BISHOPS ON ECONOMIC JUSTICE, 1986*

Catholic pastoral messages of recent years have caused controversy. The Challenge of Peace: God's Promise and Our Response *generated a vigorous debate over the proper moral response to the arms race. A second, more recent pastoral letter,* Economic Justice For All; Catholic Social Teaching and the U.S. Economy, *also precipitated a national debate. This second document was intended to add to "the public debate about the directions in which the U.S. economy should be moving." Although the pastoral was applauded by many Catholics, particularly the liberal elements of the Church, other, more traditional Catholics opposed it. The debate on this pastoral letter continues. Below is an excerpt from the letter.*

γ   γ   γ

1. We are believers called to follow our Lord Jesus Christ and proclaim his Gospel in the midst of a complex and powerful economy. This reality poses both opportunities and responsibilities for Catholics in the United States. Our faith calls us to measure this economy not only by what it produces, but also by how it touches human life and whether it protects or undermines the dignity of the human person. Economic decisions have human consequences and moral content; they help or hurt people, strengthen or weaken family life, advance or diminish the quality of justice in our land.

2. This is why we have written "Economic Justice for All," a pastoral letter on Catholic social teaching and the U.S. economy. This letter is a personal invitation to Catholics in the United States to use the resources of our faith, the strength of our economy and the opportunites of our democracy to

*Quoted in *The National Catholic Reporter,* January 9, 1987. Used by permission of the U.S. Catholic Conference

shape a society which better protects the dignity and basic rights of our sisters and brothers both in this land and around the world. . . .

6. Economic life raises important social and moral questions for each of us and for society as a whole. Like family life, economic life is one of the chief areas where we live out our faith, love our neighbor, confront temptation, fulfill God's creative design and achieve our holiness. Our economic activity in factory, field, office or shop feeds our families—or feeds our anxieties. It exercises our talents—or wastes them. It raises our hopes—or crushes them. It brings us into cooperation with others—or sets us at odds. The Second Vatican Council instructs us "to preach the message of Christ in such a way that the light of the Gospel will shine on all activities of the faithful." In this case, we are trying to look at economic life through the eyes of faith, applying traditional church teaching to the U.S. economy. . . .

12. The pastoral letter is not a blueprint for the American economy. It does not embrace any particular theory of how the economy works nor does it attempt to resolve the disputes between different schools of economic thought. Instead, our letter turns to Scripture and to the social teachings of the church. There, we discover what our economic life must serve, what standards it must meet. Let us examine some of these basic moral principles.

13. *Every economic decision and institution must be judged in light of whether it protects or undermines the dignity of the human person.* The pastoral letter begins with the human person. We believe the person is sacred—the clearest reflection of God among us. Human dignity comes from God, not from nationality, race, sex, economic status or any human accomplishment. We judge any economic system by what it does *for* and *to* people and by how it permits all to *participate* in it. The economy should serve people, and not the other way around.

14. *Human dignity can be realized and protected only in community.* In our teaching, the human person is not only sacred but also social. How we organize our society—in economics and politics, in law and policy—directly affects human dignity and the capacity of individuals to grow in community.

The obligation to "love our neighbor" has an individual dimension, but it also requires a broader social commitment to the common good. We have many partial ways to measure and debate the health of our economy—gross national product, per capita income, stock market prices. The Christian vision of economic life looks beyond them all and asks, "Does economic life enhance or threaten our life together as a community?"

15. *All people have a right to participate in the economic life of society.* Basic justice demands that people be assured a minimum level of participation in the economy. It is wrong for a person or group to be unfairly excluded or unable to participate or not contribute to the economy. For example, people who are both able and willing to work, but cannot get a job, are deprived of the participation that is so vital to human development. For it is through employment that most individuals and families meet their material needs, exercise their talents and have an opportunity to contribute to the larger community. Such participation has special significance in our tradition because we believe that it is a means by which we join in carrying forward God's creative activity.

16. *All members of society have a special obligation to the poor and vulnerable.* From the Scriptures and church teaching we learn that the justice of a society is tested by the treatment of the poor. The justice that was the sign of God's covenant with Israel was measured by how the poor and unprotected— the widow, the orphan and the stranger—were treated. The kingdom that Jesus proclaimed in his word and ministry excludes no one. Throughout Israel's history and in early Christianity the poor are agents of God's transforming power. "The spirit of the Lord is upon me, because he has anointed me to preach the good news to the poor." This was Jesus' first public utterance. Jesus takes the side of those most in need. In the Last Judgment so dramatically described in St. Matthew's Gospel, we are told that we will be judged according to how we respond to the hungry, the thirsty, the naked, the stranger. As followers of Christ, we are challenged to make a fundamental "option for the poor"—to speak for the voiceless, to defend the defenseless, to assess life-styles, policies and social institutions in terms of their impact on the poor. This "option for the poor" does not mean pitting one group against

another, but rather, strengthening the whole community by assisting those who are most vulnerable. As Christians, we are called to respond to the needs of *all* our brothers and sisters, but those with the greatest needs require the greatest response.

17. *Human rights are the minimum conditions for life in community.* In Catholic teaching, human rights include not only civil and political rights, but also economic rights. As Pope John XXIII declared, all people have a right to life, food, clothing, shelter, rest, medical care, education and employment. This means that when people are without a chance to earn a living and must go hungry and homeless, they are being denied basic rights. Society must ensure that these rights are protected. In this way we will ensure that the minimum conditions of economic justice are met for all our sisters and brothers.

18. *Society as a whole, acting through public and private institutions, has the moral responsibility to enhance human dignity and protect human rights.* In addition to the clear responsibility of private institutions, government has an essential responsibility in this area. This does not mean that government has the primary or exclusive role, but it does have a positive moral responsibility in safeguarding human rights and ensuring that the minimum conditions of human dignity are met for all. In a democracy, government is a means by which we can act together to protect what is important to us and to promote our common values.

19. These six moral principles are not the only ones presented in the pastoral letter, but they give an overview of the moral vision that we are trying to share. This vision of economic life cannot exist in a vacuum; it must be translated into concrete measures. Our pastoral letter spells out some specific applications of Catholic moral principles. We call for a new national commitment to full employment. We say it is a social and moral scandal that one of every seven Americans is poor, and we call for concerted efforts to eradicate poverty. The fulfillment of the basic needs of the poor is of the highest priority. We urge that all economic policies be evaluated in light of their impact on the life and stability of the family. We support measures to halt the loss of family farms and to resist the growing concentration in the ownership of agricultural re-

sources. We specify ways in which the United States can do far more to relieve the plight of the poor nations and assist in their development. We also reaffirm church teaching on the rights of workers, collective bargaining, private property sub-sidiarity and equal opportunity. . . .

29. We believe that the Christian view of life, including economic life, can transform the lives of individuals, families, schools and our whole culture. We believe that, with your prayers, reflection, service and action, our economy can be shaped so that human dignity prospers and the human person is served. This is the unfinished work of our nation. This is the challenge of our faith. . . .

FOR FURTHER READING

Abell, Aaron, *American Catholicism and Social Action: A Search for Social Justice, 1865–1950* (Notre Dame, 1960).
_____, ed., *American Catholic Thought on Social Questions* (Indianapolis, 1968).

Alvarez, David J., ed., *An American Church: Essays on the Americanization of the Catholic Church* (Moraga, CA, 1979).

Archdeacon, Thomas J., *Becoming American: An Ethnic History* (New York, 1983).

Bangert, William, *A History of the Society of Jesus* (St. Louis, 1972).

Barry, Colman, *The Catholic Church and German Americans* (Milwaukee, 1953).

Betten, Neil, *Catholic Activism and the Industrial Worker* (Gainsville, FL, 1976).

Billington, Ray A., *The Protestant Crusade, 1800–1860* (New York, 1938).

Blanshard, Paul, *American Freedom and Catholic Power* (Boston, 1949).

Bolton, Herbert E., *The Rim of Christendom: A Biography of Eusubio Francisco Kino* (New York, 1936).

Bowden, Henry W., *American Indians and Christian Missions* (Chicago, 1981).

Brewer, Mary E., *Nuns and the Education of American Catholic Women, 1860–1920* (Chicago, 1987).

Brinkley, Alan. *Voices of Protest: Huey Long, Father Coughlin and the Great Depression* (New York, 1982).

Broderick, Francis L., *Right Reverend New Dealer: John A. Ryan* (New York, 1963).

Browne, Henry J. *The Catholic Church and the Knights of Labor* (Washington, DC, 1949).

Callahan, Daniel, *The Mind of the Catholic Layman* (New York, 1963).

Carey, Patrick W., ed., *American Catholic Religious Thought* (New York, 1987).
_____, *An Immigrant Bishop: John England's Adaptation of Irish Catholicism to American Republicanism* (New York, 1982).

227

Castelli, Jim, and George Gallup, Jr., *The American Catholic People* (Garden City, NY, 1987).

Castelli, Jim, *The Bishops and the Bomb* (Garden City, NY, 1984).

Cogley, John, *Catholic America* (New York, 1973).

Cohalen, Florence, *A Popular History of the Archdiocese of New York* (New York, 1983).

Commager, Henry Steele, *The American Mind* (New Haven, CT, 1950).

Connelley, James F., ed., *The History of the Archdiocese of Philadelphia* (Philadelphia, 1976).

Cook, Sherburne F., *The Conflict Between the California Indians and the White Civilization* (Berkeley, CA, 1976).

Crosby, Donald F., *God, Church, and Flag: Senator Joseph McCarthy and the Catholic Church, 1950–1957* (Chapel Hill, NC, 1978).

Cross, Robert D., *The Emergence of Liberal Catholicism in America* (Cambridge, MA, 1958).

Curran, Robert E., *Michael Augustine Corrigan and the Shaping of Conservative Catholicism in America, 1878–1902* (New York, 1978).

Curry, Lerond, *Protestant-Catholic Relations in America* (Lexington, KY, 1972).

Dohen, Dorothy, *Nationalism and American Catholicism* (New York, 1967).

Dolan, Jay P., *The American Catholic Experience* (Garden City, NY, 1985).

⸺, ed., *The American Catholic Parish,* 2 vols., (New York, 1987).

⸺, *Catholic Revivalism* (Notre Dame, 1978).

⸺, *The Immigrant Church: New York's Irish and German Catholics, 1815–1865* (Baltimore, 1975).

Donnelley, Joseph P., *Jacques Marquette, 1637–1675* (Chicago, 1968).

Dyrud, Keith, et al., eds., *The Other Catholics* (New York, 1978).

Ellis, John Tracy, *American Catholics and the Intellectual Life* (Chicago, 1956).

⸺, *American Catholicism,* Rev. ed., (Chicago, 1969).

⸺, *Catholics in Colonial America* (Baltimore, 1965).

_____, ed., *The Catholic Priest in the United States* (Collegeville, MN, 1971).

_____, ed., *Documents of American Catholic History*, 3rd ed., 3 vols., (Wilmington, DE, 1987).

_____, *The Life of James Cardinal Gibbons*, 2 vols., (Milwaukee, 1952).

Ewens, Mary, *The Role of the Nun in Nineteenth Century America* (New York, 1978).

Feldberg, Michael, *The Philadelphia Riots of 1844* (Westport, CT, 1975).

Fogarty, Gerald, *The Vatican and the American Hierarchy from 1870 to 1965* (Wilmington, DE, 1985).

Foley, Albert, *God's Men of Color: The Colored Catholic Priests of the United States, 1854–1954* (New York, 1954).

Flynn, George, *American Catholics and the Roosevelt Presidency, 1932–1936* (Lexington, KY, 1968).

_____, *Roosevelt and Romanism: Catholics and American Diplomacy, 1937–1945* (Westport, CT, 1976).

Fuchs, Lawrence, *John F. Kennedy and American Catholicism* (New York, 1967).

Gannon, Michael V., *The Cross in the Sand: The Early Catholic Church in Florida, 1513–1870* (Gainesville, FL, 1965).

Geiger, Maynard, *The Life and Times of Fray Junipero Serra, O.F.M.*, 2 vols., (Washington, DC, 1959).

Gleason, Philip, ed., *Catholicism in America* (New York, 1970).

_____, *The Conservative Reformers: German-American Catholics and the Social Order* (Notre Dame, 1968).

_____, ed., *Contemporary Catholicism in the United States* (Notre Dame, 1969).

_____, *Keeping the Faith: American Catholicism Past and Present* (Notre Dame, 1987).

Gray, Francine, *Divine Disobedience: Profiles in Catholic Radicalism* (New York, 1969).

Greeley, Andrew M., *American Catholics: A Social Portrait* (New York, 1977).

_____, *American Catholics Since the Council* (Chicago, 1985).

_____, et al., *Catholic Schools in a Declining Church* (New York, 1976).

Greene, Victor, *For God and Country: The Rise of Polish and Lithuanian Ethnic Consciousness in America, 1860–1910* (Madison, 1975).

Guilday, Peter K., *History of the Councils of Baltimore, 1791–1884* (New York, 1932).

Halsey, William, *The Survival of American Innocence: Catholicism in an Era of Disillusionment, 1920–1940* (Notre Dame, 1980).

Handlin, Oscar, *Al Smith and His America* (Boston, 1958).

Hanley, Thomas O'Brien, *Charles Carroll of Carrollton* (Washington, DC, 1970).

———, ed., *The John Carroll Papers*, 3 vols. (Notre Dame, 1976).

Hanna, Mary T., *Catholics and American Politics* (Cambridge, MA, 1979).

Hennesey, James, *American Catholics* (New York, 1981).

Herberg, Will, *Protestant-Catholic-Jew* (Garden City, NY, 1955).

Heuston, Robert F., *The Catholic Press and Nativism, 1840–1860* (New York, 1976).

Higham, John, *Strangers in the Land: Patterns of American Nativism, 1860–1925*, Rev. ed., (New York, 1965).

Holden, Vincent, *The Yankee Paul: Isaac Thomas Hecker* (Milwaukee, 1958).

Kantowicz, Edward R., *Corporation Sole: Cardinal Mundelein and Chicago Catholicism* (Notre Dame, 1983).

Kauffman, Christopher J., *Faith and Fraternalism: The History of the Knights of Columbus, 1882–1982* (New York, 1982).

Kelly, George A., *The Battle for the American Church* (Garden City, NY, 1979).

Kinzer, Donald, *An Episode in Anti-Catholicism: The American Protective Association* (Seattle, WA, 1964).

Kissell, John L., *Friars, Soldiers, and Reformers: Hispanic Arizona and the Sonora Missions, 1767–1856* (Tucson, AZ, 1976).

Kuzniewski, Anthony J., *Faith and Fatherland: The Polish Church War in Wisconsin, 1896–1918* (Notre Dame, 1983).

Lannie, Vincent P., *Public Money and Parochial Education; Bishop Hughes, Governor Seward, and the New York School Controversy* (Cleveland, 1968).

Lichtman, Allan J., *Prejudice and the Old Politics: The Presidential Election of 1928* (Chapel Hill, NC, 1979).

Linkh, Richard, *American Catholicism and European Immigrants* (New York, 1975).

Lord, Robert, et al., *History of the Archdiocese of Boston,* 3 vols., (New York, 1944).

Marty, Martin, *An Invitation to American Catholic History* (Chicago, 1986).

Mattingly, Mary R., *The Catholic Church on the Kentucky Frontier, 1785–1812* (Washington, DC, 1936).

McAvoy, Thomas T., *The Great Crisis in American Catholic History, 1895–1900* (Chicago, 1957).

_____, *A History of the Catholic Church in the United States* (Notre Dame, 1969).

McNeal, Patricia F., *The American Catholic Peace Movement, 1928–1972* (New York, 1978).

Melville, Annabelle, *John Carroll of Baltimore: Founder of the American Catholic Hierarchy* (New York, 1955).

_____, *Elizabeth Bayley Seton, 1774–1821* (New York, 1951).

Merwick, Donna, *Boston Priests, 1848–1910* (Cambridge, MA, 1973).

Messbarger, Paul, *Fiction with a Parochial Purpose* (Boston, 1971).

Metzger, Charles H., *Catholics and the American Revolution* (Chicago, 1962).

Miller, Randall, and Thomas D. Marzik, eds., *Immigrants and Religion in Urban America* (Philadelphia, 1977).

Miller, William D., *A Harsh and Dreadful Love: Dorothy Day and the Catholic Worker Movement* (New York, 1973).

Morison, Samuel E., *The European Discovery of America: The Southern Voyages, A.D. 1492–1616* (New York, 1974).

Moynihan, James A., *The Life of Archbishop John Ireland* (New York, 1953).

Murnion, Philip, *The Catholic Priest and the Changing Structure of Pastoral Ministry, New York, 1920–1970* (New York, 1978).

Murray, John Courtney, *We Hold These Truths: Catholic Reflections on the American Proposition* (New York, 1960).

Nolan, Hugh J., ed., *Pastoral Letters of the U.S. Catholic Bishops,* 4 vols., (Washington, DC, 1983).

O'Brien, David J., *American Catholics and Social Reform: The New Deal Years* (New York, 1968).

Osborne, William, *The Segregated Covenant: Race Relations and American Catholics* (New York, 1967).

Parot, Joseph J., *Polish Catholics in Chicago, 1850–1920* (DeKalb, IL, 1981).

Pelotte, Donald J., *John Courtney Murray* (New York, 1976).

Peihl, Mel, *Breaking Bread: The Catholic Worker and the Origins of Catholic Radicalism* (Philadelphia, 1982).

Prucha, F. Paul, *The Churches and the Indian Schools, 1888–1912* (Lincoln, NE, 1979).

Raboteau, Albert, *Slave Religion* (New York, 1978).

Ray, Mary A., *American Opinion of Roman Catholicism in the Eighteenth Century* (New York, 1936).

Reilly, Daniel F., *The School Controversy, 1891–1893* (Washington, DC, 1943).

Roohan, James E., *American Catholics and the Social Question, 1865–1900* (New York, 1976).

Ryan, Thomas R., *Orestes A. Brownson* (Huntington, IN, 1976).

Sanders, James, *The Education of an Urban Minority: Catholics in Chicago, 1833–1965* (New York, 1977).

Shanabruch, Charles, *Chicago's Catholics* (Notre Dame, 1981).

Shannon, James P., *Catholic Colonization on the Western Frontier* (New Haven, CT, 1957).

Shaw, Richard, *Dagger John: The Unquiet Life and Times of Archbishop John Hughes* (New York, 1977).

Spalding, Thomas, *Martin John Spalding* (Washington, DC, 1973).

Sullivan, Robert E. and James O'Toole, eds., *Catholic Boston* (Boston, 1985).

Sweeney, David, *The Life of John Lancaster Spalding* (New York, 1965).

Taylor, Ronald B., *Chavez and the Farm Workers* (Boston, 1975).

Thwaites, Reuben G., ed., *Jesuit Relations and Allied Documents,* 73 vols., (Cleveland, 1896–1901).

Tomasi, Silvano, *Piety and Power: The Role of the Italian Parishes in the New York Metropolitan Area, 1880–1930* (New York, 1975).

Trisco, Robert, ed., *Catholics in America, 1776–1976* (Washington, DC, 1976).

Tull, Charles J., *Father Coughlin and the New Deal* (Syracuse, 1965).

Van Allan, Rodger, *The Commonweal and American Catholicism* (Philadelphia, 1974).

Warner, Sam Bass Jr., *The Urban Wilderness: A History of the American City* (New York, 1972).

Weisz, Howard R., *Irish American and Italian American Educational Views, 1870–1900: A Comparison* (New York, 1976).

White, James A., *The Era of Good Intentions: A Survey of American Catholic Writing Between the Years 1880–1915* (New York, 1978).

Yzermans, Vincent, ed., *American Participation in the Second Vatican Council* (New York, 1967).

INDEX